BETWEEN THE RIVERS

FLY FISHING STORIES OF THE WEST

BETWEEN THE RIVERS

FLY FISHING STORIES OF THE WEST

by Michele White (Murray), Al Marlowe,
and Karen Rae Christopherson

BETWEEN THE RIVERS

FLY FISHING STORIES OF THE WEST

© 2019 Michele White (Murray), Lake George, Colorado

All rights reserved. No part of this book may be reproduced or transmitted in any form or by any means without written permission from the author.

"Everybody needs a secret fishin' hole. A person needs one even if they don't fish,"

(Al Marlowe, 2017)

CHAPTERS

1. Joe's Bar in Craig, Montana (by Michele White "Murray") 1
2. The Get Away (by Al Marlowe) 13
3. The White River (by Karen Rae Christopherson) 26
4. Rude Fish of the North (by Michele White "Murray") 35
5. Sour Toe of the North (by Michele White "Murray") 47
6. Take Yer Own Igloo to Alaska (by Michele White "Murray") 58
7. Lizzy's River (by Michele White "Murray") 66
8. Winter Fish Dreams (by Michele White "Murray") 77
9. DKNY on the Colorado (by Michele White "Murray") 87
10. Between the Rivers (by Michele White "Murray") 95
11. Binkler's Butterball (by Michele White "Murray") 111
12. Floating the Beaverhead in a Wooden Tub (by Michele White "Murray") 127
13. Fly Fishing a Super-Fund Site: Butte, Montana (by Michele White "Murray") 138
14. Salmon Flies on the Colorado (by Michele White "Murray") 152
15. Cochetopa Creek 163
16. Autumn on the Dolores: An October Odyssey (by Al Marlowe) 168
17. The San Juan River below Navajo Dam, New Mexico (by Michele White "Murray") 179
18. One of Those Days (by Al Marlowe) 194
19. Ride Through the Clouds (by Al Marlowe) 199

20.	Al's Designer Humpy (by Al Marlowe)	209
21.	Fishing the "Un-hatches" (by Al Marlowe)	218
22.	The Flat Tops Wilderness, Colorado (by Al Marlowe)	225
23.	Fly Tying (by Al Marlowe)	234
24.	High-Tech Fly Fishing (by Al Marlowe)	242
25.	Stealth Fishing (by Al Marlowe)	246
26.	The Fishing Pole Thief (by Al Marlowe)	256
27.	Fly fishing the Futa - A Trip to Chile (by Karen Rae Christopherson)	264
28.	Whitewater Fly fishing (by Karen Rae Christopherson)	271
29.	I Wanted a Fishing Dog (by Karen Rae Christopherson)	278
30.	Elmo the Fishing Snob (by Michele White "Murray")	286
31.	Mid-October on the Gunnison River (by Michele White "Murray")	296
32.	River Calves (by Michele White "Murray")	312
33.	Propelled by Desire (by Michele White "Murray")	320

INTRODUCTION

These are fishing stories by three authors about places, boats, bars, trucks, dogs and people. They occur in Colorado, Montana, Wyoming, Nevada, Idaho and Utah and other fishable parts of the world.

Michele White (Murray) is a geologist, fly fishing guide, and owns Tumbling Trout Fly Shop in Lake George, Colorado. She and her spouse (also a geologist) have been fly fishing and rowing a dory for over 20 years.

Al Marlowe is also a geologist and writer. He and his wife have been casting flies and lures into streams and lakes all over the West for more than 40 years.

Karen Rae Christopherson is a geophysicist, writer, and has been fly fishing since 1970. Karen has written for several fly fishing publications and co-authored many maps and books with Al Marlowe. She is the webmaster for coloradofishing.net and wyomingfishing.net.

"Between the Rivers" is a compilation of humorous adventures that happen on the road, in the middle of the journey, in the campsite, at the bar, and during the fishing trips. These are tales in common with most fishing people, with travelers, with mountain folk - in short, these are tales of living the dream.

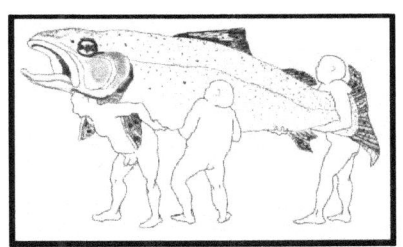

1. Joe's Bar in Craig, Montana (by Michele White "Murray")

"A train story on the Missouri River, whether or not you expected one."

Who thinks Dwight Yoakam is a whiner? The folk at Joe's Bar in Craig, Montana do. Joe is a distinguished older gentleman of the same caliber charm as Bob Hope: gentle, witty, talented, but with red hair. The local patrons are charming, too, (though I wouldn't get on the wrong side with them). We first met these friendly people as the result of our prehistoric motor home (with shag-carpeted ceiling like a space ship in a B-rated movie) suffering yet another mechanical breakdown in a saga of ongoing mechanical failures on the road. On this leg of our journey, we ended up sitting at a bar having the best Bloody Mary's in the world at Joe's on the Missouri River – multiple Bloody Marys that is – directly across the tracks of a rail road line that appeared to be abandoned.

That morning, I had been standing in the Great Missouri River fishing using bead-head pheasant-tail nymphs to cast in a cascading riffle between braided sand bars. Smooth cobbles camouflaged an army of hungrily-munching brown trout that were rising to the surface like popcorn in a pan of hot oil. Our two old dogs balanced their front paws on our dory's gunnel waiting for the day's venture, faithfully guarding our lunch. I imaged that we would get in the dory soon and leave our motorhome with its newly leaking fuel pump for the shuttle driver to discover. After all, he was charging us a stiff fifty bucks to get our rolling-motel-from-hell delivered down the river to the take-out.

Fishing a riffle in the Missouri River.

My huzbun was still in the motorhome, sitting woefully behind the steering wheel in his waders. Both of his rods were rigged and waiting for him in the boat. All systems go. Yet, he sat pondering what kind of immoral life we would be leading if we left the limping motorhome for the shuttle driver to deal with. He gave in to moral obligation rather than to fishing glory. We re-hitched the boat t our motorhome and headed for town.

If your motorhome ever breaks down anywhere in west-central Montana, you should try to make it to the town of Craig. They have a mechanic there, (Ray), who keeps 20-year old Chrysler parts in stock. We watched Ray step out of somebody else's motor coach onto steps that magically appeared and then disappeared from under the chassis. We were humbled. We use a medium size hammer to whack our steps into and back out of the iron slot they live in under our door. We were elated when Ray stopped what he was doing and began to work on our hillbilly vehicle. My wonderful spouse suggested I go to the local bar and wait for him there, considering the owner and locals are known for their hospitality.

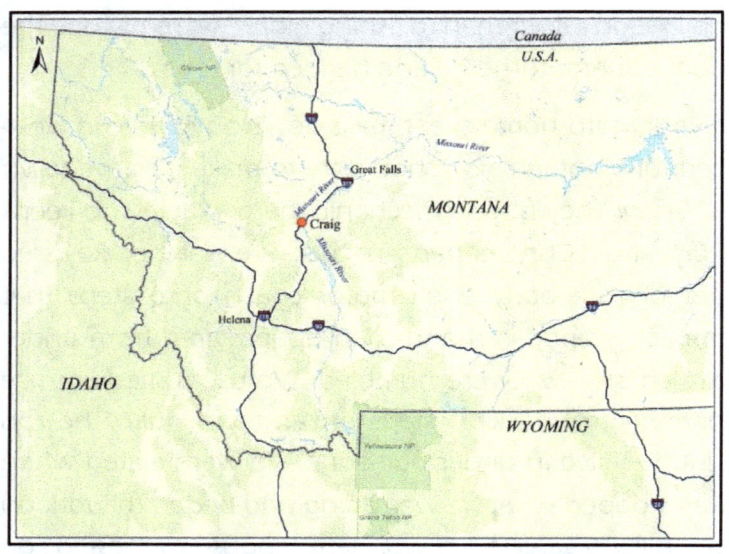

Craig, Montana on the Missouri River.

Joe's Bar is a hub for sophisticated humor, the kind your dad would like. In addition to a barrage of third generation paper copies of clever sayings tacked all over the walls like, "If your wife calls and you're not here, YOU tell her," and, "You've only got one liver – so live 'er up!" they also have the best light switch I've ever seen in a ladies' room. The switch cover is a plastic Superman with the lever sticking out of his crotch in either the up or down position. There are red rings of different colored lipstick kisses on the wall around the switch. I'll never go fishing in Montana without my lipstick again!

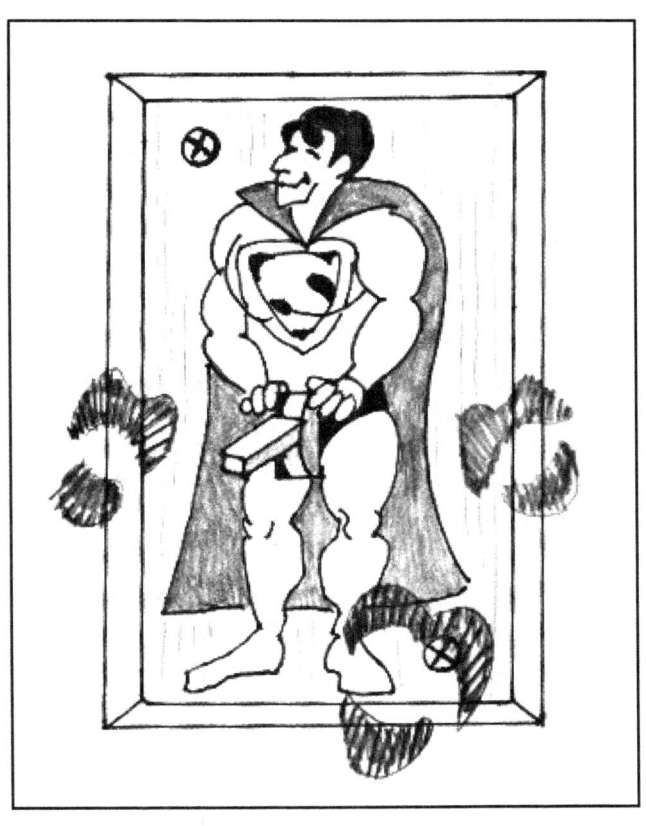

Superman light switch in the ladies' room.

Another amusement in Joe's Bar is the result of a New York Times article critiquing the fly fishing along this stretch of the Missouri River. If you sit at the bar and show any interest in fly fishing, someone will eventually bring the article to your attention because of an error the journalist made about some guy's horse. The article, though flattering about the torpedo-size fish to be had in the river, made reference to, "an old gray mare" –

probably for local color, I am guessing. This horse was actually, "a blue-roan stud", which makes a significant difference if you are the owner of said horse – which, I am guessing the bartender was. Further, the critter has since been "cut-proud" meaning one of his two-McNuggets was gone and the other was intact.

Ray (the mechanic, remember?) replaced our fuel pump in the time it takes a person to consume two Bloody Mary's. However, for the rest of the summer our motor home continued to suffer from uncanny problems (chassis separating from the floor, wiring shaking loose -- eventually, two fenders peeled off of their rivets when we were driving over Monarch Pass, Colorado <u>and</u> the U-joint simultaneously broke off its hinges forcing us to coast downhill for 6 miles with no transmission and metal fenders-a-flappin' in the wind from our flanks like Dumbo's ears).

As a result of suffering too many stressful situations of owning the motorhome, by next summer, we returned to the Great Rivers of the North in a brand-spankin' new F-350, full crew cab, SUPER-heavy duty, 12-ton, power-stroke-you-to-the-moon turbo diesel-guzzling PARTY-barge <u>with</u> an enormous new camper. The combined length of truck, overhanging camper and dory in tow was 38 feet! Plus, when our NEW vehicle developed an electrical problem on its virgin road trip to the Missouri River, we headed right for Craig (and right for Joe's Bar).

Our problem with the new truck was that it wouldn't shift out of park, though it would start. We discovered this malady while blocking an entire fueling island and the main entrance to a gasoline station just west of Great Falls. The station attendant, who used to work at a Ford dealership, suggested that our truck wouldn't shift due to the fandoogled digital brake sensor blowing a fuse due to an electrical short circuit in the wiring harness somewhere between the bumper and North Dakota. So, in order to get shifted out of park, (and to thereby clear his gas station island for the growing traffic jam waiting to enter the premise) we had to keep flipping new fuses into the appropriate slot of the fuse-box, (as was demonstrated to us by a knowledgeable paraplegic passing by the pile of vehicles in his wheelchair.)

After clearing that obstacle, we diverted our course westward to Craig where we knew we could count on the reliable mechanical service of Ray, (the guy who had fixed our 21-year old motor-home with a leaking fuel pump the summer before). And, as before, we knew that when we are having an engine problem near Craig, it's best to wait for Ray to perform his miracles over a Bloody Mary at Joe's Bar next to the abandoned train tracks. Besides, it was August and the temperature in western Montana was over 100 degrees – too hot for fishing.

We found Joe's Bar to be wonderfully dark and cool for our hot tempers (we were not happy with our new truck.) Sensing our foul mood, Joe produced from under the sink an old, small acoustic guitar with plastic strings – the kind your dad might have put under the Christmas tree when you were a kid. Apparently, everybody at Joe's Bar can play the guitar. Big, mean-looking guys and little sweet-looking guys traded the guitar and played and sang old ballads by Gordon Lightfoot, Eddie Arnold, Hank Williams Sr., and many other almost forgotten but still vaguely familiar tunes (including "On Top of Old Smokey" with the original words – NOT the errant meatball version.) We sang like day-care children in Joe's Bar in the middle of the afternoon, drinking Bloody Mary's, beer and whiskey with only a few other anglers, losing track of time. Joe's Bar is, in that sense, a timeless place, good for letting go of one's worries.

That's maybe why I parked our rig on the train tracks. It was 104 degrees (Fahrenheit) in the shade that day and everything in western Montana was on fire except for trout fur. (I had caught some Brown trout with singed eyelashes, obviously the result of feeding on burning mayflies the day before.) It was way too hot for fishing or even just floating down the river under the hot sky. You couldn't touch your beer without searing your lips. My reel had vapor lock. The sun beat down on our heads like a tired old elephant's butt. There was no respite in dunking our hats in the Missouri River. Along the shore, professional outfitters parked their dories to let their glum clients hide in the shade of cattails, futile lines hanging limp over the gunnels.

We didn't think we could take our dogs into Joe's (though I've never asked), and as I said, it was a really hot day. I could tell by their deflated, molten bodies that the dogs didn't care if I left them to melt into poodles on the back seat of the truck during Ray's repairs. I rolled the windows down for public appearance to look as if there was a breeze for them to enjoy.

Though Ray fixed our truck in 15 minutes, I didn't want to get back out on the hot river. So, Joe told me to park our rig under the shade of an enormous, uncontrolled elm in his front yard next to the bar. I tried to park there but the top of our camper made a crushing noise, threatening his living room window by bending the huge tree's branches back. Still, there was no shade on the dogs. I saw that not too far from the bar was another large elm casting a fully available shadow across a nice flat-looking place about the size of our Ford land-barge. I scoped the scene for practicality: no driveways would be blocked if I parked there. I saw only the old train tracks that were mostly obscured by dry, dead, knee-high weeds. Obviously abandoned.

So, I parked our brand spankin' new truck-house and dory in tow under the OTHER elm in its magnificent shade away from Joe's Bar. The dogs were unconscious panting in their dreams about having gone to Dog Hell and being forced to chase rabbits on fire without any water. I left them in that state.

When I returned to the bar the patrons were fashioning an enormous caddis dry fly out of a beer bottle and a bent spoon with some straws. We were way into our 30th round of campfire songs, Joe was yodeling cowboy style as the guitar got passed around and people sang and laughed and drank and told jokes and the afternoon was really going very well, when I heard a train whistle. A TRAIN whistle. So, I asked the cozy group in general,

"Hey – does a train still run through here?"

They all answered that *'yes,'* once in a while a train does come through here.

So I asked to no one in particular, *"Does it run on these tracks right outside of the bar?"*

Now, I had my huzbun's attention (he's pretty sharp). They said that there was only one set of tracks. And I said,

"I'm talking about those weed covered, abandoned tracks."

"They're not abandoned", patrons answered.

"WOO-oooo-WOOOOO!!!!" said oncoming train.

My darling huzbun quietly asked me, *"Michele, where did you park the rig with the dogs and dory?"*

The train whistled yet again but much closer now and I stood not so quickly as to alarm anyone but my 'bun was faster than me and he disappeared through the door quite rapidly. I didn't want to witness any pending events in action but I went outside also to be available should an unforeseen catastrophe suddenly arise.

In a short while, the train came rattling by and produced a mild breeze. I was surprised to see that the sun was still up – always an uncomfortable discovery when you've been drinking all day. And there were the doggies, all tongues and tails lolling out the window of the crew cab in the shade of Joe's elm, having been moved by a simply astounding huzbun only moments before.

My wonderful 'bun rejoined the festivities in Joe's Bar with a perspiring face. He ordered another beer before he would even look at me again. Joe had complete confidence in his ability to woo any woman by yodeling, (he was looking awfully cavalier and suave with his little guitar and gallant eye.) Though I'm particularly partial to older men who can yodel, he had no idea of the heroic feat performed. Bun not only delivers me to and from rivers in Montana, he also delivers me from catastrophe.

We ended up sleeping in the camper right where "bun" parked it in Joe's front yard at a safe distance from the train tracks. The next day, we continued fishing rivers and streams amidst Montana's inferno, grateful for a good mechanic, good people, and great Bloody Marys at Joe's Bar. In particular, we are grateful for slow locomotive engineers who have enough foresight to anticipate that a large truck, camper and boat might be parked on their tracks outside of Joe's Bar on the Missouri River in Craig, Montana.

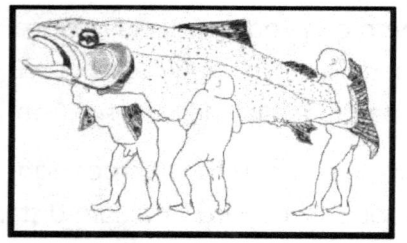

2. The Get Away (by Al Marlowe)

"Everybody needs a secret fishin' hole. A person needs one even if they don't fish."

A secret fishin' hole is not necessarily a place to just fish. It's a place to get away. Not as in running away, just to get away. A person running away has to keep on running. A get away place is a place to retreat. It's a place to retreat from the daily pressures of life. It's a place to spend some quiet time alone.

Difficult access is not a requirement for a secret fishin' hole. It doesn't even need to be a place no one else uses. All that's necessary is that in this place, a fisherman can isolate himself from the rest of the world. Over the years, I have had several secret fishin' holes.

To qualify as a secret fishin' hole, it should be a place that is not well known. It should be a place the fisherman has gone to some effort to locate and investigate. Ideally, it will be a place offering a reasonable chance of fishing success. If the fishing is poor to non-existent, it would just be a secret hole, not a secret fishin' hole.

A secret fishin' hole doesn't need to be miles from the nearest road but that seems to be the case most often. It should be a place that is so good a fisherman will tell only his closest buddies. If a fishing hole must be shared with three-hundred other fishermen, it's hardly secret. As a reader, you should feel privileged since I'm sharing it with you.

The best time to visit there is in the spring. Late May is a good month. To get to it, just go west from my house. Then, after driving about an hour, head north for a few miles, then go west again. When you come to a good dirt road, follow it south about three miles and park by a small stream. From here, it's only a two and one-half mile walk.

On the way, walk quietly. Many times, I have seen elk before they knew a human was around. You may see a cow with a new calf, the fourth or fifth she has raised, teaching it everything an elk needs to know to grow into a big bull. Or teaching it how to be a good cow and raise more calves of its own.

Elk watching Al watching them watching him.

Sometimes, I scare up a deer, perhaps a buck with the beginnings of his new antlers. He will pause for a moment before he determines that a human must be a threat, and then retreat to his secret hole. If I have been quiet, I may see him before he sees me, and he will continue his deer activities undisturbed.

A Mule deer watching Al watching him watching him.

My secret fishin' hole is often accessible by the middle of May. At an elevation of about 9,000 feet, the winter's snows have almost gone, and the moist ground is covered with a carpet of new wildflowers. The earliest to appear are dandelions. Yellow seems to be the predominant color on my first visit of the new season, as various tiny, five-petalled flowers cover the wettest areas, making it difficult to walk without crushing their fragile shapes.

Melvin watching Al watching him watching him.

In June, cinquefoils will add more yellow to the area. By mid-Summer, scarlet gilias, Indian paintbrush and many other flowers will add their various colors and hues to the landscape. In other places along the trail to my secret fishin' hole, blue Pasqual sprout from sandy soil.

The trail is easy. It leads through pine forests and aspen groves. In this season, the aspens have just begun to bud. The fuzzy catkins mean that winter is over and the trees will soon be green again. My walk takes me through a grassy meadow where I might by chance spot a coyote family foraging in hopes of finding a mouse or even a snowshoe hare. Off to the side of the trail, the crumbling remains of old log buildings bear witness to the harshness of a century of winters.

An unexpected historic cabin to investigate.

Now, the last gentle grade has been climbed and I begin a short descent through sagebrush down to the creek. I pause to search the surface of the first beaver pond for signs of fish feeding in the clear cold water. Seeing nothing for now, I continue on up the trail past other ponds. The winter has taken its toll on the watershed. A fragile dam stands waiting for the beaver corps to repair a breech washed out in the spring thaw that sent a torrent of water down the narrow drainage. Another pond is murky with sediment from the broken dam.

I continue along the trail and cross the three-foot wide stream, stepping on granite boulders to stay dry. In a shallow brush strewn pond, I see the first sign of activity as a six-inch brookie viciously slashes at a tiny gray insect. A dozen fresh-cut aspen poles indicate that the beavers intend to repair the damage to their structures done by winter's melting snows.

Occasionally, as I approach a pond on the stream, I am startled as a pair of mallard ducks erupt from the water, telling me in no uncertain quacks that they object to my intrusion on their solitude. I guess they prefer to make little ducks in the privacy of their own secret pond. The ducks share their home with the beavers, the dam-building rodents responsible for the ponds. Muskrats also enjoy the fruits of the beaver's efforts.

At the end of the two and one-half mile walk is a spring, flowing perhaps three gallons of cold, pure water per minute. At a constant year-round 38 degrees, the water is thirst quenching. It bubbles up out of a small fracture in the diorite, a granite-like rock and adds its small flow to the tiny stream feeding my secret fishin' hole.

While the walk in was not long, the day is warm. As I sit near the spring, I eat a sandwich and wash it down with the near-frozen elixir from the spring. I toss the crust to a begging camp-robber bird that carries it off to store in his secret cache of tidbits, saved for his rainy day. The brookies have just started to rise, feeding on nearly invisible insects, as a hairy woodpecker searches for larger insects in the lodgepole pine trees that are over abundant.

My stomach no longer complaining and my thirst satisfied, I am now ready to attend to serious business: fishing for brookies in my secret fishin' hole. Today, I brought my spinning rod, so will start with a yellow Rooster Tail, one with black spots on the body, a spinner that has accounted for many trout in these ponds.

In many ponds, the fish are extremely wary. So wary, that it is necessary to approach and cast with a low profile. The ponds of my secret fishin' hole are an exception. The fish just don't care if I'm not hidden. After a few casts near the beaver house with no results, I move to the next pond, one that is a little larger and deeper.

I cast near the remains of a much older beaver dam, now submerged, the result of a newer, higher dam these industrious animals have constructed. The older dam now only has the remains of a few willows and coarse grass growing on it, enough debris to promptly snare my spinner as it becomes hopelessly tangled in the brush. That was my last yellow Rooster Tail. It really doesn't matter, though, so I tie on a brown one, one with a bit of yellow in the feather that covers the treble-hook.

A Rooster Tail lure works best when retrieved just fast enough to make the blade turn. It is even better to reel in a couple of feet of line, then pause to let the lure sink a few inches, then retrieve again. This often results in a hit as the spinner falls, tumbling like an injured fry, or whatever the brookies think it is. Who knows what is going on in their little pea-sized brains?

Examples of Rooster Tail lures.

After seventeen casts, the line becomes taught as a fifteen-inch male takes the fake food. Having caught fish in the six to eight-pound range, the pound-and-a-half brookie seems easy to bring to the net. But that's not important. This fish is special. I caught it in my secret fishin' hole. No one else is around to see me land it. No one is here to crowd me. The only person here besides me is the friend with whom I share the experience, you. And even though no one is here - no one but Melvin, my Golden Retriever, and you - to watch as it is returned to its home the experience is special.

Melvin waiting for his master to do something interesting for a dog.

As the cool of the morning now releases its grip on the thermometer, the afternoon warmth fills the beaver meadow. The heat from the sun penetrates the water in the ponds and insect activity increases. The pond's surface, which had been calm, is now filled with tiny rings, made by trichoptera (caddis fly) emerging from their larval cases in which they have spent the past two or three years. As the adult caddis struggles to be free of the surface film, the effort is noticed by a cruising fish and an insect that has survived for many months on the pond's bottom now helps fill a trout's belly, even before it can make more little caddis to feed more brookies.

Eventually, the fish lose interest in my spinners, and they actively slurp down insects emerging on the surface. I decide to switch to flies. As I dig through my tackle, looking for a plastic bubble and some leader, I am startled as a red shafted flicker, a woodpecker common here, begins drumming on the trunk of a lodge pole pine, searching for lunch. For such a small bird, they can make a lot of noise.

Finally, I have succeeded in making the transition from lures to flies, just in time for the cumulus clouds that have been building in the west to peel out their first drum-roll of thunder. The air, which has been calm so far, now begins blowing in gusts that makes casting nearly impossible. As the first drops of rain fall, I franticly search for my rain coat, which I discover was left in the truck, nearly three miles away. Fortunately, the shower is light and brief, yielding just enough moisture to dot the ground with microscopic puddles; not so much as to put down the feeding brookies.

After two or three casts, a brookie takes my fly. Melvin is alerted by the splashing of the terrified fish and as I release it to make more little ones, he gazes at the circle in the water where it disappeared and wonders how a fish does that.

The fishing has been good today in my secret fishin' hole. I failed to tally my catch. Statistics aren't important at my secret fishin' hole anyway. I did keep a few smaller ones for the skillet. I return to the spring for a final drink before walking back to camp. Along the way, an inviting pond persuades Melvin (my golden retriever) to take a swim. As he approaches a pond, he is surprised by a beaver neither of us has seen and we both react with surprise as his paddle-like tail sends a geyser of water three feet in the air. Though curious about this strange critter, Melvin decides to find another pond for his swim.

The sun has now started its journey to the other side of the world. We step up our pace. Camp is still two miles away. Colors fade in the dimming light. As I follow the trail, Melvin searches the brush on either side. He finds many interesting smells in his secret place that need to be investigated as only a dog can investigate.

We get back just as a hint of evening coolness begins to diffuse through the air. As we walk past a tree, thoughts of fish frying in the skillet are interrupted when an obnoxious pine squirrel scolds us for being too close to his secret hole. A robin chirps his evening song, a more pleasant sounding refrain than the mindless chatter of a mindless squirrel.

Melvin and I sit on the ground by the fire. Melvin utters sounds of contentment while I enjoy a beer. Off in the distance, a coyote howls as he emerges from his secret hole to begin his search for dinner. The eight-inch brookies curl as they react to the heat of the oil in the frying pan. I'm sure better things could be prepared for the evening meal but I'm also not certain what it would be. Accompanied by beans, bread and beer, supper has been a feast, shared only by Melvin and you.

We relax by the fire, which is growing smaller. I reach for another log and hesitate. "*It's kinda late*", I tell Melvin. The fire provides just enough light to find my way into my sleeping bag. Melvin crawls into the tent and lies down beside me. Just before sleep comes, we listen to the night sounds of silence. I recount the events of the day in my secret fishin' hole as I drift off.

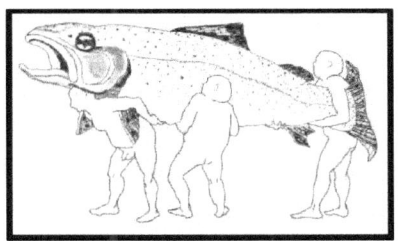

3. The White River (by Karen Rae Christopherson)

"When it's not your average stream fishing situation."

I had been seeing pictures sent to me by my friends of insanely HUGE cutts (cutthroat trout) and cutbows (cutthroat and rainbow trout hybrids) of lengths over 20 inches plus caught on the White River by Meeker. I too wanted to have my chance at catching one of these beautiful fish. Finally, we found four days to make the trip to the area and try our hand at capturing this reward. Yes, there truly are large cutthroats, cutbows, rainbows, and whitefish on the White River.

The White River originates in the Flat Tops Wilderness Area of western Colorado in Route National Forest. The North Fork of the White River starts at Trappers Lake; the South Fork starts just a few miles south of that. They meet up at a confluence near Buford and form a gorgeous freestone river traveling through a broad valley of hayfields.

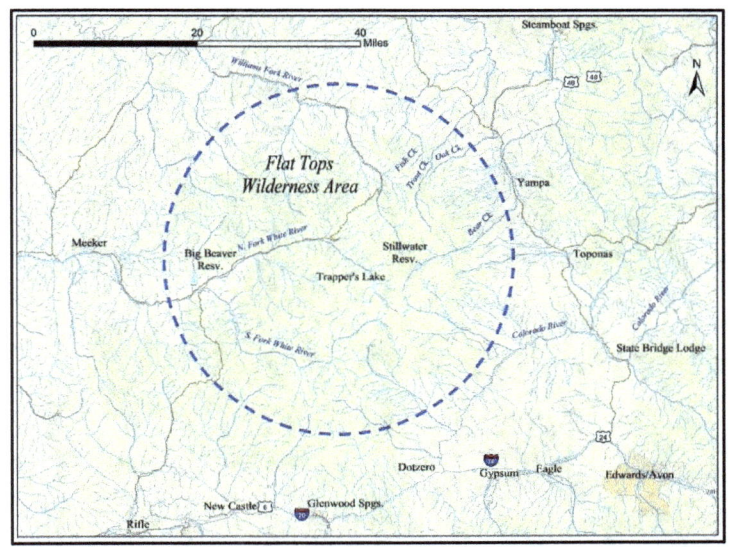

Flat Tops Wilderness Area in Colorado.

Fishing along the South Fork next to a wall of limestone.

There are very nice public access points on the White River. Anglers can fish the major river for several miles between Meeker and Buford. The South Fork has less public access except for a section within the Flat Tops

Wilderness Area. Luckily, there are 20 miles of river to follow with a foot trail alongside and the gradient is manageable (an average of 2.5% drop). Unfortunately, there are very "willowy" sections and access is limited to beating a path through thick brush to reach the river. Once on the bank, an angler can wade in the water for most of the public sections and then look for a decent spot to exit.

Casting to pools on the South Fork - you'll spot fish in the feeding lanes. The challenge is to tempt them with your fly!

Dry flies and nymphs work equally well when fishing seams and riffles along the main stem of the White River.

We came to this river not just to catch fish – we wanted to catch really large, gorgeous fish like my friends had been catching. We decided to camp in our trailer at Sleepy Cat Guest Ranch so that we could enjoy their private fishing access to 2.5 miles of the South Fork of the White River just upstream of the confluence with the North Fork of the White River. Plus, this resort is located within a reasonably short drive to other public access to the river.

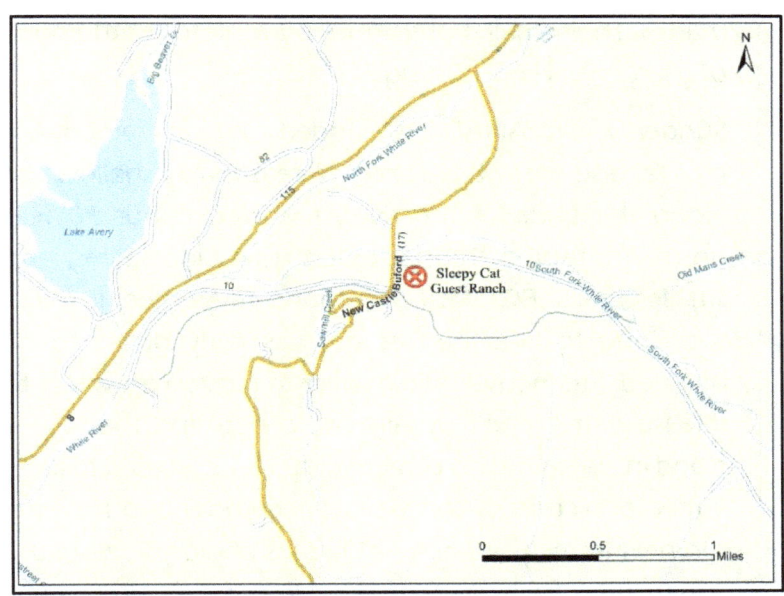

Location of the Sleepy Cat Ranch relative to the South and North forks of the White River.

Upon arrival, I pleaded with the husband to please take care of setting up the camp and looking after our Lab without me so that I could go immediately to check out the fly fishing. I selected a size 14 H&L Variant with a small bead-head pheasant-tail dropper (my semi-standard rig when I don't know what else to use). Then, I left him.

Almost immediately (probably within 20 minutes or so) I had landed several rainbows and whitefish. The whitefish were especially fun. They certainly took the dry flies with enthusiasm but setting the hook was a different matter. Their small mouths make it hard to set the hook of a large fly. I kept casting.

Suddenly - **NIRVANA!** First, I landed a 20-inch rainbow - a nice fat one. He was waiting in a reasonably shallow run along the bank of the river. I waded about 30 feet upstream, fishing the narrowed runs, side seams, and smaller riffles. **BOOM!** I had found my whale. It didn't take long to land him as he was fairly docile to be handled. I maneuvered him over to shallowest water to release him (I don't usually use a net) and then I just stood in awe. With no camera or audience, I tried to keep a mental picture of this beautiful cutbow and held my rod next to measure him - 23 inches of glory. One of the largest fish I have ever landed. He released easily and I remained in a state of shock and reverie for hours while re-telling the story to my husband and dog over several G&T's (gin and tonics).

The next day we hiked up the South Fork in Flat Tops Wilderness. The trail is easy to hike and follows closely to the river. After about two miles, we found a spot where there weren't too many willows and we could hike to the bank fairly easily. It was very nice water of a manageable size to wade and crystal clear. We started wading in the river. Within a few minutes we came to an attractive bend in the river that just shouted to us, "*Fish here, perfect spot*" - you know - one of those outer river bends that has logs and deep pools of calm water with foam.

I suggested to my husband that he fish it first - he deserved this prime opportunity for having let me disappear to the river the previous day while he set up camp and looked after the dog. Now, he began to cast but shortly snagged his line on an overhanging limb. Rather than spook any fish out by tugging at his line, he quietly called to me to try casting into the hole. I cast a few times and then had a strike on the nymph. I cast again and I got him!

Pretty soon I realized this was not your average smaller stream, high altitude kind of fish. This serious animal took off and gave me quite the practice session in landing a large trout. I was glad I had decided to bring my 5-wt rod instead of my normal lighter weight, packable rod. After minutes of suffering great anxiety, I finally landed him, again sans net. I had to have a picture of this guy. I carefully unhooked him and held his slippery body up for the husband to get a shot via zoom lens from across the river. We estimate this cutt was about 18 feet –um inches - long and he certainly was healthy! I was happy – I'd caught BIG fish!

Working a large trout from the bank.

Karen with a nice fish on the White River.

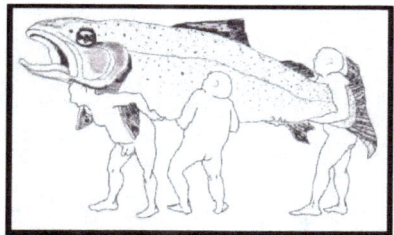

4. Rude Fish of the North (by Michele White "Murray")

(How to avoid catching really big fish in Alaska)

The large, milky-white rivers of the North looked like volcano barf. Their swollen, mineral-laden waters flooded the open plains as if the Earth had belched its innards out. We were terrified of their immense proportions. Root-balls of upturned trees stuck out of the rivers vibrating in the powerful current here and there, strewn higgledy-piggledy across the nearly half-a-mile wide girth of desolate flood-plain, like ghosts of a forest destroyed by some catastrophe.

We both read Anthony J. Route's book, *"Flyfishing Alaska,"* (revised edition), which portrayed the huge rivers of Alaska as fertile and hosting abundant giant fish. Mr. Route was dauntless in his suggestion to use heavy silver lures and brightly colored yarn streamers to attract the aggressive salmon from the murky depths if we dared. However, each margin of the swollen rivers threatened to swallow us alive when we approached. The tall banks were composed of unconsolidated cobbles and sand. They trembled from the flooded current gouging away underfoot. If the banks were to crumble away, only the moose and caribou would know of our demise (and a caribou doesn't care-a-boo about you.) Despite the potential for deadly disaster, we ventured into the braided meanders of the river's torrent with huge, over-sized rods originally purchased for fishing the coastal surf of Mexico. We hefted fat metallic lures with sharp treble hooks, brightly-colored fiber streamers, and an abundant variety of wet-flies to snare a salmon. After two days of trying: no luck. There were no great fishys in the North fool enough to accept our pathetic decoys.

"*We're skunked, man!*" That was the disparaging conclusion from my companion (brother-in-law), Dillon. "*How could a fish live in there? It looks like oatmeal.*"

We returned to the rental car and spread the mighty reference book on the hood. Dillon read to me aloud:

"*Says right here, '...the first look at the seemingly opaque water of a glacially-colored river brings disappointment. They [anglers just like us] think the river is blown out, unfishable. Nothing could be further from the truth.'*" Dillon followed the printed word with his finger as if seeking absolution. He continued:

"*Obviously, visibility decreases in glacially-tinted water...use larger patterns...a size 2 Black Woolhead Sculpin...or chartreuse...when fishing glacial waters, many fishers employ a method called attractor-yarn technique...brightly colored piece of yarn tied to a leader about 2-feet ahead of a more somber offering such as a nymph...' Hmmm...ends with a warning about wading with caution in glacially-silted water... ' Might end up over your head...' "*

I wasn't listening anymore. I had my powerful digital camera out and was on a mission to capture the butt end of a bald eagle sitting on a branch of a dead tree directly overhead. They were everywhere – thick as pigeons – the bald eagles.

That stop was one of our many repeated frustrating fishing experiences s as we drove on a circuitous route from Skagway's flooded fjord above Juneau to Delta Junction, Alaska. We would be meeting up with my huzbun at the Clearwater Lodge and then continue our fishing journey up through Alaska and over to the Yukon of northern Canada to Dawson City and return to Skagway via Whitehorse. We wanted to catch steelhead, King Salmon, Sockeye Salmon, Pike – all the great fish of the North.

Everything in this part of the world seemed extraordinarily huge and vacant. The lakes were like seas. The forests were uncut. The plains unfenced. Horizons were uninterrupted without power lines or even contrails of airlines passing over the rest of the world's surface. Each river seemed larger and more swollen than the last. Dillon tied long ribbons of yellow and red twine to his line to no avail: not a bite anywhere.

"*Whoa!!*" I woke from a start in the front seat. Dillon was braking the car hard for a dark shadow that leapt across the road in front of us and flew like a wisp of smoke into the woods. It was late in the day but the sun was still shining – a perpetual presence in this land of the Midnight Sun.

"*Did you see that?*" He asked. "*It must have been someone's dog, like maybe a German Shepherd or something!*"

I glanced at him to see if he was joking. He wasn't. He was still looking with big eyes to where the animal vanished. I said, "*I don't think there is a dog running around out here. I think we just saw a WOLF!*"

"*Really? You really think that was maybe a wolf?*" He asked me.

"*Maybe,*" I answered. As it turned out, we saw the ass-end of a lot of exciting the animals. We saw the backend of a moose, the haunch of a caribou, and this was probably a wolf's rear end.

During our journey, there were multiple times when we braked for an animal on the side of the road, even eagles, or simply stopped at grand views that stirred our hearts. However, despite our upstream jaunts, we never once saw a bear.

By the end of the first week on the road of this no-fish-in-hand journey, Dillon had devised a cunning technique: He took a large (#4) stimulator pattern (that is a fuzzy, colorful dry fly found particularly appetizing to a snacking trout) and tied approximately 24" of orange twine above the fly. With great care, he spliced together a fat leader of heavy fishing line and the combination of fly / orange twine. Then, he meticulously applied a fine amount of viscous floatant (schmoo) to both the fly and to the leader taking care not to muss the fine ends of the spliced center. When this operation was accomplished, he stuck a chunk of hot dog on the hook and threw the wad by hand into the river as far as he could toss the mess like a meatball. He refined this method and eventually abandoned using any fly at all, just a plain old treble hook with a hot dog. Basically – we were bait fishin'. However, we still didn't catch anything. Not even a glimpse of a fish's sniggering snout.

"I don't get it. Are we supposed to be using hand grenades or something?"

Our frustration was growing. For most of the road trip, I couldn't have asked for a more benign, easygoing, comrade than my brother-in-law. Dillon was unassuming, uncomplaining, and a trooper except for the leg of the journey when our gas gauge was reading near empty and the next town still loomed 15 miles away. He was so distracted by the steadily dipping needle below "E" that I feared he would steer off into the

Tioga forest from distraction. I took over the helm and placed a music cassette over the fuel gauge so he wouldn't focus on it. When the little gas-tank light went on, I put black electric tape over that.

"You've got to trust me on this – say we get 15 miles to the gallon at the least – a carton of milk is a gallon, so imagine a gallon of gas. We have got to have a about a gallon of milk worth of gas so there has got be at least 10 miles worth of go left in our tank. We can dip at least a quarter-of-an-inch below empty and there has still got to be a coffee cup of juice left in the tank before we truly run dry. I think we can make it no problem," I said.

That is my usual take on running low on gas. I have only ran out of gas one time in my life and even then, after I let the engine sit overnight on I-25 north of Gallop, New Mexico, enough vapor had condensed gas in the tank to start the engine up and roll us forward five more miles to make it to the exit ramp, which I coasted down and rolled into the gas station.

Dillon and I are normally competent, patient anglers. We were just not familiar with fishing rivers of this monstrous size, being Colorado natives after all. So, when we came across more manageable streams along our route through the Great North we pulled the car over to the side of the road and sought zealous vindication with smaller creeks. Dillon attached a big canister of bear spray and a pound of cow bells to his vest prior to hiking up the banks of the smaller tributary streams in the vicinity of the greater rivers. We angled with our more common-sized gear in these smaller, clear creeks, all the while whistling and yakking for the sake of scaring bears. We yelled the "*Marco-Polo-Buddy-System*" back and forth to each other through thickets along the way (You yell "MARCO" and if your buddy hears you, he replies, "POLO!!!" to keep track of each other and let the bears know exactly where the yummy fishermen are wading).

A sign warning of bear issues.

When we finally arrived at our destination, the Clearwater Lodge at Delta Junction in central Alaska to meet my huzbun, we had to admit to him that we just spent 4 days fishing the Great Rivers of the North in pristine wilderness and not had a single bite. We were desperate to catch a steel head salmon.

"You're way too early for the Salmon. They won't be running up this far north until the end of the summer and even then, only the Kings, the Chum, and the Silver Salmon make it this far into the interior. The Steelhead stay near the coast."

We were flabbergasted! (Apparently, we didn't read that part in the master book.)

"Don't worry, though, the Clearwater River is known for the Grayling and there are Dolly Varden here too," he added pointing to the lovely, quiet stream flowing in front of his cabin.

Before Doug left our home in Colorado for his month long reconnaissance of the region, he had tied a pile of special gray Parachute Adams dry flies that we normally use back home on the South Platte River. He now gave each of us a handful of these special flies. I noticed the pattern differed slightly from our usual ones by a distinct contrast of using both black and white hackle with added copper ribbing to the thorax. They were extra bushy, too. With this succulent-looking fly, Dillon and I stepped into the crystal clear water of the – you got it – Clearwater River, and finally began catching fish – new species to us: grayling and Dolly Vardens.

We spent our first evening with all three of us standing in one bend directly across from the grassy lawn of the bar at the lodge with only about two-arm lengths between each other, casting and catching the bubbly lips of grayling that teamed in the current. The fish were everywhere – even underfoot like on the San Juan River below the Navajo Dam in New Mexico. They slipped around our ankles. I tried not to kick them in their faces but when we released them they hung out between our feet. The sun never sets in the summer, but the dinner bell does go off in the belly. Eventually, we reeled in our lines and began the return trip by wading upstream to where the water was shallow enough to cross safely. A very large lady moose entered the river directly across from us and blocked our way. She was stared intently at us. We blinked back at her.

"Stand still together. She shouldn't charge a group of humans," Doug cautioned us. However, the moose seemed annoyed that we were standing exactly where she wanted to cross. It was a stalemate.

The big moose.

"*OK. Let's go downstream slowly,*" he said and we followed behind him. The moose made a parallel path on the opposite side of the river also following us. So, we headed upstream again and were finally able to cross the river but the moose was then grazing in front of our cabin door. We had no choice but to go to the bar.

"*Oh, her?*" replied the bartender. "*That's the camp moose. She won't hurt you. Was probably just watching you fish.*"

For the next couple of days, we stayed at the lodge and reveled in the abundant fish to be caught. The Dolly Varden look a lot like brook trout but they do not have blue dots or orange fins. At that time of year (June) in the smaller streams like the Clearwater, the Dolly Varden were not very big – tiny actually – being only about 6 inches (or less) in size. However, the zippy little things were amazingly aggressive and would leap from only a few inches of water to take a fly the size of its head. Basically, if a Dolly Varden can get its mouth on it – it's going to eat it. The Dolly Vardens would commonly take my fly when I was not paying attention, for example, when I was simply looking for signs of fish rising and letting my line drift down river. They are kamikazes of a fish in that way.

The grayling, on the other hand, are an emotional bunch of fish. I was sitting on my butt in my waders half-submerged in the water with my legs sticking out in front of me nursing a hang-over. I let my special Parachute

Adams of Doug's unique design float under willows on the opposite bank (a mere 10 feet across from my outstretched feet at this location of my rather supine posture) and watched grayling rise out of the shadow of overhanging grass to pounce on my fly like a cat on a mouse. They threw themselves in aerial assault to smother the fly with flat slaps of their bodies (must be why they have sails for dorsal fins, which they actually do). Then, with sudden astonishment, they would look shocked to realize their snack was attached by a thin line to a lady wearing rubber pants sitting in the water.

Graylings only fight for a moment before feinting from disbelief. Even after release, you have to hold them under the surface and apologize gently until they get over it or they'll just float away upside down with hurt feelings. I let one go between my legs while I was still sitting in the water and he stayed inside my thigh-corral thinking about what had transpired. Eventually, he forgot why he had been so upset in the first place (a newt may be smarter.) I released him from this containment by spreading my ankles apart and sticking a finger in his ear.

Despite an ominous beginning, the over-all ambiance of our fishing trip turned out to be spectacular after all. Sometimes life experiences are subtle that way. A precocious person (especially me) needs to be humbled by the wilderness and skunked from time to time. We entered Alaska with expectations of grandeur and with intent to conquer the Rivers of the North as savvy anglers from Colorado. However, the size of the rivers daunted us and the salmon weren't even there yet. Only the silly graylings were to be wrangled by the bushel. As austere as the Alaskan rivers remain, they still call to us. We can hear their thunder in the North Wind. I think when we return, we will try to go later in the year when the King Salmon are actually running.

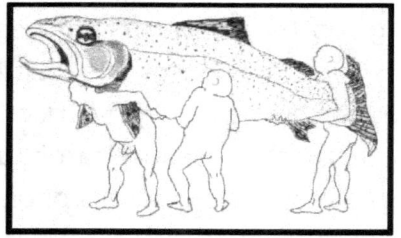

5. Sour Toe of the North (by Michele White "Murray")

"Adventure Bar of the Yukon"

It was supposed to be a purely south Alaskan-bound trip but we wandered way farther north and east than originally intended. Our path neared the tip of the planet where gravity pulls on your senses and the sun swivels around in the sky on an errant path between aspirin, beer, fishing and tormented naps hoping for sleep that never comes. After six days wandering the Great White North in a Buick LeSabre, we eventually arrived in Canada's vast Yukon Territory. "We" being myself and Dillon (my 24-year old brother-in-law). We wanted to check out the great city of Chicken, Alaska along the "Top of the World Highway". Like most other bored Americans, we were looking to fluff our pitiful lives with some substance derived from travel adventure.

"Chicken", in case you might miss it.

Directions to the central business district.

They never found the poor thing.

If I said, 'We had no idea what to expect,' I would be lying. We expected Chicken to be exotic. We sought the bizarre. Unfortunately, Chicken was a disappointment and there was a large, old guy in dirty underwear sitting on the deck of the only store, so we didn't even stop. However, in Dawson City, Yukon we met, "The Sour Toe of the North". That stupendous evening made the whole trip significant.

The Toe is a real toe - a human one of the big toe variety. A long, yellow, wretched toenail verifies the neglect, age, and loneliness of its original bearer prior to being severed from a frostbitten foot. Now, this toe is desiccated, preserved (not petrified), and venerated by designated keepers or "Captains of the Toe" at the Sourdough Saloon in Dawson City. Purpose? For five American dollars, you can put this toe in your cocktail, drink the swill down until Toe touches your lips, and earn by means of shocking display, prominent respect (or not) accompanied by aghast sighs from onlookers. The Captain of the Toe takes your money, fills out an official certificate of authenticity as to your lewd act, replaces the toe with great ceremony in a child-sized casket and the people disperse.

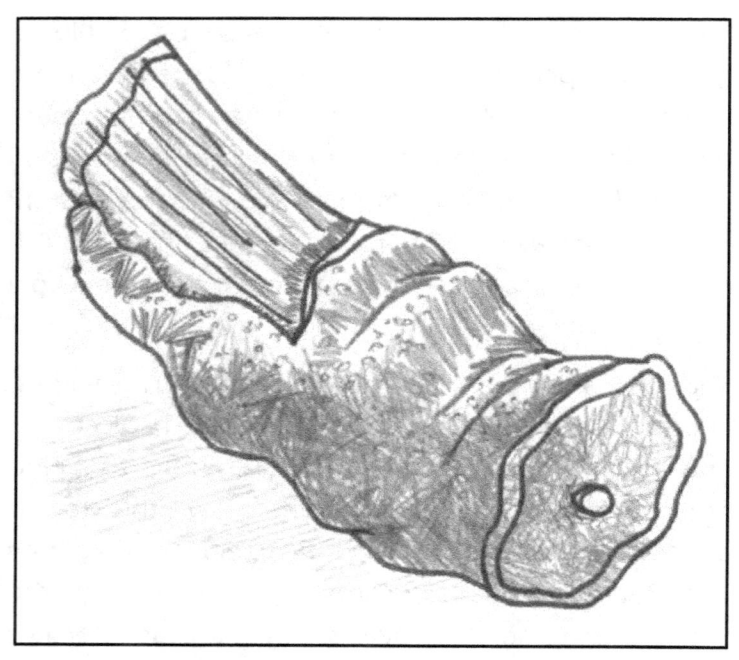

The horrible, offensive appendage.

Dillon and I found NOT the TOE so much as the PEOPLE who kissed the toe to be kind of scary. As a matter of fact, the toe itself (once dried and replaced in a jar of coarse salt for preservation) wasn't that bad to handle (though, the toenail like I said, had been neglected in its past life to the point that I felt nauseated to imagine the old man – obviously not a woman – who never trimmed his nails or cared for personal hygiene. One can only speculate.) I did not touch the toe but Dillon and the cute bartender, Molly, did handle the thing in order to flaunt its horror. (I traded metallic implements with Molly for beer at the bar. There is a silver bassoon reed plaque in this image.)

Implements of silver to pay for the beer.

At this tippy end of the planet, the Earth's increased gravity plays with one's mind. So does the constant daylight. Neither of us wore a watch and we could only tell by the behavior of people, whether it was day or night. If people went to bed – it must be night. We would lower our voices to pretend it was night but we couldn't sleep. We pitched a tent and put ourselves into sleeping bags, but actually only napped fitfully when fatigue finally knocked us over BECAUSE THE SUN WAS UP!!! And gravity? We found that the pull of Magnetic North in such close proximity to our hearts was aligning the iron in our hemoglobin to the orbit of the Earth. If it weren't for gravity and the increasing density of our proportioned bodily masses, we and the other tourists would have spun off the face of the planet, scattering like human debris in the cosmos, I am sure.

It was in this state of mental entropy from lack of sleep, that we discovered the sensitivity of the tourists to booze. We came from a higher elevation and that factor apparently contributed to our survival. We could drink like fish and yet stay out of jail. We discovered this physical propensity to swill large amounts of alcohol at the Red Dog Saloon in Juneau where we found that the bleary eyed tourists from the luxury ocean liners were eager to play a local game called "Tablecloth of the North," which supposedly originated in Chicken, Alaska.

To play Tablecloth of the North two teams clasp tablecloths at chin height and try to flip by any means cloth napkins onto the other teams' tablecloth. If a team can move all of their napkins onto the other teams' tablecloth, then the losers have to buy a round of drinks. It's an ancient Inuit game originally played with caribou skins and narwhal tusks.

Dillon and I were making this game up, pulling facts of its origin and rules out of our butts in order to stimulate the drinking and consequent spending of money on behalf of our friend, Sam the Bartender, who was stuck in the mire of these poor tired tourists' stupor. I happened to have two of my mother's tablecloths and napkins from Aurora, Colorado as the source of this imaginary game. I intended to give these cloths to Kitty, a Juneau friend who has so many cats she has to replace her tablecloths often. My mother was going to toss the tablecloths when I remembered Kitty and then toted the tablecloths back to Juneau. Kitty did not meet with us and so the tablecloths found their way to the Red Dog Saloon with a bunch of bored tourists sitting in front of my friend, Sam, like I said, the bartender...

After initiating The Tablecloth of the North Game so easily in Juneau, Dillon and I realized we had Power over people. We found we could control an entire bar by keeping a straight face and telling a bizarre story because tourists (like us) are desperate to witness or experience a unique adventure in the NORTH. Thus, we understood of the phenomenon of drinking with a TOE in Dawson City because we had founded our own folklore about the tablecloth game in Juneau.

Due to our resilience to the pull of Magnetic North, (and resilience to fictitious bar folklore) the toe's only effect on us was to make us curious as to its true origin, which was relayed to us by a huge, friendly, ex-felon placer miner who befriended us at the saloon. We like him. He was a charming man, and I personally believe there might be a grain of truth in some of the things he said. Here is my recounting of, "The Official Toe Story":

The Toe is NOT a drinking game. That would be illegal in Canada. It is a historic icon, such as Jack London, famous author of the Yukon, who once lived in Dawson City. The original Toe had been stolen and abused beyond repair to the point the Sourdough Saloon has a couple of replacement toes, now, in reserve. People with frostbite donate them on behalf of Dawson City's economic prosperity. (Our large friend's eyes met with the bar owner's son, Matthew Van Norstrand's eyes for verification of Toe story integrity. Matt nodded affirmation. Mr. Charming ex-felon continued...)

Apparently, there are other bars that try to mimic the Toe with other frostbitten appendages. ('Thumbs, for example', he told us.) Dillon and I speculated as to other more interesting body parts. Isn't there a drink called "slippery nipple"? Bar owner's son, Matt, interjects, "The Toe is ESTABLISHED!" And theirs [Sourdough Saloon] is the official toe.

Interestingly, the Sourdough Saloon doesn't own the Toe. They lease it. And, they're not the first. Before them, the Klondike Visitor's Association leased the Toe from Bill Holmes, who bought the rights to the Toe from Riverboat Captain Dick Stevenson (you might arrive Dawson City by riverboat, even today, because you have to cross the Yukon River by ferry if you arrive via Chicken from the west like we did.) Captain Stevenson found the toe in a jar in the wall of an old miner's cabin.

The crossing over the Yukon River to get to Dawson City.

Apparently, the loss of a toe (or any frostbitten part of a body) was not uncommon amongst the "Cheechaka" (Cree word for newcomers who had not experienced an Arctic winter.) The opposite of a Cheechaka is an old "Sourdough" – or person seasoned by experience enough to know how to keep a leather pouch of flour warm around their neck for the live yeast to survive. The yeast cultures were the source of subsistence on self-rising bread: sourdough. Twenty-five years ago, Captain Stevenson recognized the Toe's potential as a curiosity (like our Tablecloth Game of the North, I suppose) and christened the appendage: "The Sour-TOE of the

Sourdough." Subsequently, he also initiated the first "Captain of the Toe" augmented with his riverboat captain's cap (the original cap accompanies the Toe, today, and is stored in the child-sized casket along with the Toe and the certificates.) The rest is history.

The Toe hit the Road. Captain Stevenson took the Toe to Whitehorse where it was displayed and venerated in the local newspaper. The Toe toured on a regular circuit, including Watson Lake, Tok, Chicken, and Ft. Selkirk. It wintered in Faro. Captain Stevenson retired from the Toe Tour by first leasing, then selling it to Bill Holmes – one of his mates on the original river ship. Bill's family almost let the Toe go, until the Klondike Visitor's Association offered to lease the Toe. Eventually, Dick Van Norstrand (Matt's father who owns the Sourdough Saloon) acquired rights to lease the Toe. At one time, our narrator friend tried to buy the Toe but it was a no go on the toe. Now, the Sourdough Saloon is where you will find the Sour Toe of the Sourdough.

The evening never ended. How could it? The sun never sets! We closed the Sourdough Saloon and followed the ex-felon to another bar, saw spectacles there also. By the time Dawson City was verging on another dawn, (we could tell by the wild tourists' behavior) too many kooky fools were wobbling around the streets looking for another adventure in the realm of extremes. With Molly the bartender, Matt the owner's son, the ex-felon and one drunk Indian (of a nearly extinct Athabaskan nation) named, Baloo, begging us to stay, Dillon and I ran to our car. We both felt we couldn't get out of there fast enough. We drove into the woods south of town and hid from the eternal daylight in our tent, hoping to catch an elusive dream, evidence of having fallen asleep at last. It took us two days of fishing to purify ourselves and shake the jitters from Dawson City and their Sour Toe of the Sourdough.

Too much fun but not for us.

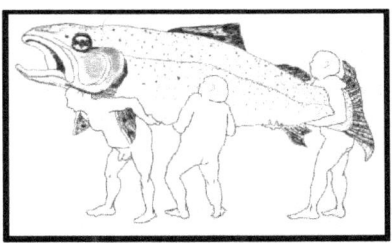

6. Take Yer Own Igloo to Alaska (by Michele White "Murray")

"Cool Gear for the Educated Traveler"

My huzbun was working in central Alaska and I was going to join him there for a fishing spree. I love to pack for journeys and adventures. I've been doing this for a long time because my parents are military. Additionally, I commonly commute for long distances dating from way back when I was a rambling youth so my choice of travel gear has evolved with experience for functionality and efficiency. As a result, I commonly use an ice chest as a piece of luggage. This trip, however, my bun will be probably be surprised by the fine cooler I found.

When I was a college student, I bonded with a medium-sized, Nuagahyde, monkey-vomit brown suitcase. I snagged it from my parents' basement. They bought a matching set, as had all the other military families on Xanadu Street, from the BX (base exchange). During that time (the Vietnam Era), Aurora was a suburban triangle established between Fitzsimons Army Medical Center, Lowry Air Force Base, and Buckley Strategic Air Command. When I grew up in Aurora, it was a little town sprawling no further east than where I-225 now lies. There used to be an archway over Colfax Avenue that said, "*Welcome to Aurora – Gateway to the Rockies*!" though we kids had no idea what the Rockies were.

I played the bassoon for my escape from Aurora plan. The bassoon is heavy – much heavier than a flute, which I often wondered why I had not taken up flute, or oboe, or piccolo – anything other than the case of bricks my instrument felt like when I shouldered the case by its strap. I would drive my brother's car from Aurora to Boulder and park near campus. Then, I removed a little red wagon from the trunk for toting all of my gear (bassoon, books, music stand, etc.) to my classes. The rolling duffle bag had not been invented yet nor hidden back-pack straps on a soft gig-bag. Just trudging with a load. That's how ya did it.

After I dropped out of college (I don't know if I actually dropped out or got "diss-enrolled" for going AWOL before final exams but the timing of the severance with my educational institute was, as the least, mutual). I packed my Nuagahyde bag for Albuquerque and began commuting between Albuquerque and Denver because I owned a French-Macro-biotic Creperie in Albuquerque, played the bassoon in Denver, and had an ass-hole cowboy for a boyfriend in Albuquerque with an apartment in Denver. I went bankrupt quite shortly thereafter. My monkey-vomit-brown suitcase disappeared in the desert tied to a white mule ridden by a German journalist. I met this man when he was hitch hiking with a dog from Santé Fe to Albuquerque. He borrowed my luggage bag and I never saw him again but I received a photo of him riding cross country on a white mule. I then moved to NYC to continue being a bassoonist with a different borrowed suitcase from my parents' newest set: maroon, collapsible, all-in-one luggage that contained 8 inter-fitting pieces ranging in size from gigantic to large to medium to small all the way down to a toiletries ditty bag. The whole bundle only cost $19.99!! I snagged the medium one.

NYC is a lonely place for a girl from Aurora. I flew home every holiday. My parents visited and subsequently needed their own luggage – all of it. So, one Christmas they gave me my own new green one of the latest in travel design. It was medium-sized, semi-hard exterior that was covered with fabric. The most significant feature, though – totally state of the art – was that it rolled on wheels and had a detachable tug-along-leash to pull it through the halls of Stapleton International Airport. The rolling suitcase revolutionized my travel but, the industry of Travel Gear was just about to explode exponentially, as was my world.

It hadn't occurred to me that I had spent most of my life in front of a music stand with a double reed hanging out of my mouth until I met geologists. These people did not stay in the city. They hiked in mountains and backpacked. Through my geologist friends, I acquired my first sleeping bag (EMS brand) and back-pack (REI had just come out with soft-frame packs.) These geologists took me with them to the Grand Canyon where I saw my first river dory and wild women wearing water sandals and river dresses. I saw my first Patagonia rain gear, my first neoprene bottle, Tiva sandals, zip-off convertible hiking pants. When I got back to NYC I finished both my music and my geology degrees and moved back to Colorado – but not to Aurora – I needed to learn what the Rockies were about. I was a geologist now and while I finished my Master's degree I took to living on the Colorado River in a small red clown car across from State Bridge Lodge (SBL). I bought my first ice chest: a Coleman. It had a trap door in the lid to keep the contents cold when extracting a beer. I began to use the cooler for holding my cook gear when I traveled.

That was decades ago. I continued commuting for all my jobs (SBL–to-Boulder for my graduate degree; Sonora, Mexico-to–Boulder for my thesis study; Edwards-to-Denver-to–Nevada for the Yucca Mountain Project; and then on to work in Peru, Alaska, Indonesia, Finland, W. Africa, and beyond...) Today, in my home office without even going downstairs to the basement or looking in the closet, I know I have 3 different sized rolling duffle bags with internal weather-tight bladders, water resistant zippers and removable external storage systems. I have assorted colors / sizes of dry bags for the river, including a clear one. I have multiple wheeled backpacks of varying sizes with detachable daypacks and hidden shoulder straps. I have two wheeled office totes with reinforced padding for laptop and removable zippered pouches. Most of my gear has hidden back-pack straps, retractable handles, cargo departments, zippered security pockets, water-proof, neoprene, removable gear pouches, with rod tube holders, water bottle clips, and compression straps. We own several simpler gear bags for horse tack, hockey, fishing, kayaking, skiing, hunting, and dog stuff (duplicates in some cases, for "his-n-hers".) But especially – we have multiple sizes of coolers.

Which brings me full circle: the most efficient, functional piece of travel gear I can recommend to anyone going anywhere on this plane is a big, plastic, rolling ice cooler – the kind with a retractable handle. I strap it shut with river ties (straps with the metal clamps on the ends you use on the river to hold your stuff to a raft.) And what have I got in my cooler to take to Alaska? Well... in my big blue Igloo cooler for Alaska, you will find:

- 1 Sleeping bag / 1 Pup Tent / 2 Therma-rests;
- Enamel coffee pot (packed inside with mocha coffee mix, herbal tea, packets honey in baggies);
- Back-pack stove (no combustible fuel, though, buy that at your destination);

- Water filtration system;
- 2 Forks / 2 spoons / 2 plates / 2 mugs / 2 bowls (cuz I'm meeting my huzbun);
- Anti-bug juice / sun screen combination (in a baggie);
- Collapsible cookware (stuffed with individual baggies containing Band-Aids, gauze pads, medical tape, cortisone, Neosporin, aspirin);
- 2 wide-mouth plastic water bottles stuffed with 1 hot pad, hand-towel, dishrag, scotch guard pad, steel wool;
- Small chopping board / folding buck knife;
- Carpenter's Bag (sectioned), holds Salt & Pepper, multi-spice dispenser, olive oil (transferred to a small plastic bottle inside a baggie), small table cloth, glycerin facial soap bar (in baggie), Dr. Bonner's biodegradable dish soap (in baggie), hydrogen peroxide (in baggie), mini-binoculars, duct-tape, black electric tape, batteries, stumpy flashlight / lantern combo, Q-tips, alcohol wipes, chapstick, toothpicks, Alka-Seltzer, rubber bands, hair-bands, bear bells, bungee cord, Percocets, a big Ziplock bag containing folded foil, flattened roll TP, 10 folded paper towels, 2 garbage bags, 2 lids for sealing canned goods, 2 bandanas;
- Small zipper pouch with 2-in-1 shampoo, nose spray, toothpaste / brush, sex-gear, earrings, hand lotion;
- Burlap rock bag with spatula, long fork, tongs, ladle, can opener with cork screw (business ends sheathed);
- Orvis fishing waders / boots / gravel guards;
- Assorted socks / undies stuffed into cracks and crevices; and
- One extra, folded gear bag for transferring stuff into on the return trip home;

NOTE: Anything with the potential to make an icky mess gets put in an individual baggie.

We've used coolers as luggage before but my bun has not seen this fine one. My new one is an Igloo – a big blue one, (15" x 14" x 16" interior), which is larger than a common cooler but smaller than a mini-fridge. I will check this strapped cooler through to Anchorage as my one pieces of luggage. In Anchorage, I'll rent a car and drive north. I will buy groceries and bring them to the car in boxes. Then, I'll transfer my gear to the boxes and put the food (and beer) into the cooler. If (when) we catch big salmon, we'll freeze them in the hotel's freezer, then fly them home in the – you got it –cooler. Our gear that came in the cooler will return home in the extra, folded gear bag that came in the cooler.

PS: *When I arrived at the baggage claim in Anchorage and the baggage carousel was filled with every other bag being - A COOLER!*

Big Igloo cooler and little Igloo cooler.

Take yer Igloo everywhere.

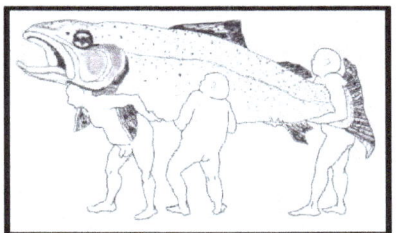

7. Lizzy's River (by Michele White "Murray")

"When friends share the same passions, their good times can mingle beyond their own generation and live on as a legacy."

One of our annual pilgrimages for fly fishing is the Big Horn River in southeastern Montana where it runs through the Crow Indian Agency below the Big Horn Canyon from the Yellow Tail dam. This is a special place not only for the gold medal quality fly fishing habitat but also for its sweeping beauty. The river is wide, easy to navigate, and amazingly clear with banks opening to vistas that look like African Savannah – wide open grass plains that stir the human heart. Along these banks, gigantic cottonwood trees tower from the plains' margins, lurking over the river's edge where tall grass marches directly to the brim of the sunny horizon. Wildlife, such as mule deer, river otters and even pheasants plus a plethora of water birds, such as cranes, pelicans, osprey, and giant blue herons are a common site. However, the fishing action is so gratifying that the beauty is almost a distraction. The fishing, actually, is our passion's destination.

The Big Horn River below the Yellow Tail Dam in Montana.

It always amazes me how little preparation we need to put into this annual trip to the Big Horn, because we have this trip down to science. Our intensity grows with anticipation as we arrive near Ft. Smith in Montana where we purchase our out-of-state fishing licenses, pay for a shuttle, and always ask what fly pattern to use. They always reply the same, "*Sow-bugs and black caddis.*" We buy a park permit at Yellowtail Dam and put our dory in below the spillway. That's our last action as common folk. When on the Big Horn, we are transcended into superhuman trout-stalkers.

There is a nagging, slight heaviness in my heart, though, when I visit the Big Horn River now, because of the memory of a friend long gone – a woman who was particularly dogmatic about this annual, trout-hunting expedition. This otherwise modest woman became as intense about fishing the Big Horn as her equally annoying black Labrador dog when presented with a tennis ball. She was locked into a Big Horn trance. My demur friend only drank beer when on This River. Usually rather pristine in her dress, she only wore frumpy clothes on This River. Mostly, though, she had a characteristic way of hailing momentary events with the same nasal declaration which <u>always</u> started with, "*You know...*" – as if some whiney old grandpa had possessed her soul in order to pass on wise old sayings to the rest of us bored girls.

I've watched this silly woman stand intently with her fishing line held between her forefingers in anticipation of the exact spot she always casted to before the dory even pushed off from the launch-site below Yellowtail Dam. Her eyes were glued to the current looking for a specific seam on the water. On her face, would be that incredible grin I associate with The Big Horn. It's an irresistible response. Lizzy grinned like a dizzy baboon as soon as the dory was buoyant, which didn't tone down even after dark when a late dinner was stuffed into her mouth. Still, that idiotic grin would beam out from between smacks of pasta, cookies, and beer – even if it was pouring a freezing rain and all our camping gear was wet. The Grin of Big Horn was upon her and she would say, "*You know, life doesn't get much better than this.*" (As if this thought was unique only to her.)

Along the lines of actually catching fish, every famous trout lair on the Big Horn has been mentally mapped into the minds of thousands of fanatic river devotees. Fisher-persons, like professional guides, the locals, and Lizzy, knew which lair would be coming up around the next bend like pilots navigating to a homing beacon. Lizzy directed me to put the boat onto a fish as if we were preparing to dock with the space station. There was no option with her: we were there to catch every single fish that might be had.

The Big Horn is the first river I've fished on where I could no longer hold my rod up due to fishing fatigue, even if I simply wanted to take a moment and appreciate my surroundings: the Big Sky Country, the clever osprey, the sentient weather, which seemed to understand our mortality and the frailty of us thin-skin-bags full of people jelly and bones floating down the river, rowing in a boat, life feeling very dreamlike. Oddly, that is usually when caddis start coming off so thick they crawl into your mouth, your eyes, your bra, your ears and you cannot help but fish with zealous fervor renewed – "*You know, you just don't care!*" said Lizzy.

Three Bald eagles (two young ones) waiting for us to pass below them on the Big Horn.

We once rowed the dory into an eddy because big fish were visibly sipping at the surface there. Overhead was a large cottonwood tree with three bald eagles sitting on a low limb over the water. The mature one had a large fish in its talons and the two younger ones were squawking with a terrible plight. It became obvious to us that these were two young eagles squawking at their mother. They wanted the fish she held in her talons but the mother wouldn't let them have it. We watched this lesson in life from below them in the eddy. The mother eagle's instincts told her that if she let her unhappy offspring have her fish that they would be doomed. She had to sit there with them screaming in her face and she had to let them suffer and feel frustrated until they figured it out on their own: the fish are in the water – go grab one for yourself. That was probably a confusing situation for an animal mother: let her babies suffer and don't give them the fish. I wondered about that emotional conflict. Human mothers have the same decisions to make sometimes I am certain.

I've floated The Big Horn with Lizzy in miserable sleet, biting hail and lightening praying for God to save us from being electrocuted. We've prayed from fear, cried over arguments, and laughed at grace and beauty on this river together, far from our families, from our lives and our worldly thoughts and worries. Once, when the oppressive heat of a stagnant summer afternoon made me feel too woozy to stand against the knee rests, I sat cross-legged on top of the bow and simply dropped my line in a dead drift with a sleepy sow-bug over the gunnel. In that moment of physical drainage, I caught a fish that ended up running the river, emptying the spool of my reel multiple times as I reeled the big fish in and it ran again to the sound of, "*ZZZZZZZzzzzzzzz...*" When the bow of the boat turned downstream because I was being pulled by the racing line, Lizzy said, "*You know, that's got to be a snag or something.*"

"*No, I can definitely feel it's a fish,*" I argued. My comrades took turns gently touching the line and debated whether it was a submerged log bouncing along the river bottom or a great hog of a trout or carp or even a turtle. When the line ran upstream, though, they believed! In a while, other folk joined us along the bank to watch the battle. After a half an hour I could no longer hold my tip up. I was exhausted. I waded inland, trying to drag the trout to the shore. When it came near the bank, Lizzy tried to sneak the net under its great body. She touched the tight line and it snapped. We stood in silence looking at my dead rod. I was relieved the struggle was over. Another boat drifted by and the guide said to the pile of spaghetti where my reel had been disgorged at my feet, "*A big one, huh?*"

Author with a big one on.

I've been amazed every time I've gone to the Big Horn at the things I've seen. There is a particular eddy with foam to provide camouflage for the trout to hide under where we like to drop the anchor. One time, Lizzy and I were mesmerized as we watched the growing relationship between one of the other anglers and a rude trout as she cast a caddis dry fly to its nose. The animal was saying, "*No. Not quite yet, silly human being.*" We could see from its snout, that it was big as a raccoon – certainly as clever. Her casts grew more complex – delicate in their lift from the surface, sublime in their aerial ascent, ever so clean and strategic where they landed. She let it drift a little to the left, then a little to the right. She cast as if the trout would eat out of her hand. The trout seemed to like that. It said, "*Now, just a little more drift. Let it swing wide for me...*"

We were lost in our observation of this ballet – the light of day beginning to change in angle, golden rays, piercing our eyes through a cloud of the tiniest midge flies hanging in the air like fairy dust – when the trout (a mighty Rainbow) took her dry fly and exploded like a maniacal bronco doing crazy cartwheels across the water coming directly at us and it wasn't stopping. The size of the critter and the abruptness of its unpredictable snatch caught us off-guard. It flung itself like an attacking boomerang at the dory and smacked into the side of the boat like a whirling dervish. Lizzy and I were so alarmed that we spontaneously screamed and grabbed onto each other. After a long, knee-slapping laugh, we were in tears. We decided to design and market trout deflectors for river dories.

"You know – that's not a bad idea!" Lizzy said.

That was how it was with Lizzy. There is another particular place – an island in the middle of a confluence with thick, deep meanders of braided channels – that is known for holding a number of predictably generous trout lairs. Upon approach, Lizzy's ever-present grin diminished with concentration. She anticipated the stroke of the oarsman and the arrival of hull on sand. She would step out of the boat, one foot on the gunnel and another foot landing on the island before the dory even grounded – not missing a stride in this assault of "her spot".

She was a bit of a bore in that respect. No one else of us fished there. She would stand chest deep in this hole catching <u>all</u> the trout. She had a long, ongoing relationship with a particular Brown trout there – a big guy. Long, muscular, dark and mean. He was <u>her</u> fish. I've watched Lizzy with screwed-up eyebrows trying to cast exactly to The Big Guy over and over again. Once, I heard a discouraging word from her normally clean mouth when she was not pleased with herself over luring this fish. When we finally moved on, it was only after she had wrangled him and touched him lovingly with her hand, releasing him with great respect. She caught that same fish, I think, every year.

There is another place we reserved for one of Lizzy's tenacious points of focus. I have multiple photographs of her standing in the same place with the same trout after the same cast in differing lights of day, differing weather, from slightly different perspectives but always with the exact same crazy grin. Year after year – exactly the same. Now, when we pass this lair without her, I still see her standing there grinning with that poor fish waiting to be released until we've taken his annual picture. Now, I leave that fish there unhindered for her, a tribute to fine times.

I've never known anyone who enjoyed fishing as much as this woman enjoyed fishing the Big Horn. I've fished with her on other rivers. I've fished with her surviving sons. There is no comparison.

"You know, that may be one of life's unpredictable pleasures – appreciating the moment, the person, even the future, though you might already have a sense that the moment at hand is already slipping into the past." But that's OK. We don't need to capture everything, put it in a box and hang onto it in anticipation of losing one's best friend. For me, all I have to do is go to the Big Horn River. I will always see her there.

The Big Horn River is banked with vintage Chevrolets chassis.

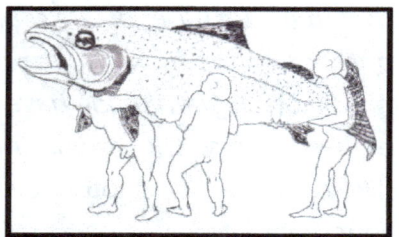

8. Winter Fish Dreams (by Michele White "Murray")

"For those days when you need to go fishing even if it is only in your mind."

There was a lot of banging coming from the far end of the house where someone was sawing, hammering, and cursing a row of new shelves for stowing fishing gear into the wall. At my end of the house two cats and one black Labrador are creating a nest in a pile of fresh-cleaned laundry in the middle of our bed. No one wanted to go outside, not even the animals, because it was many degrees below zero and an arctic blast was blowing wind-driven snow into tall ranges of migrating drifts across our yard. Deep winter had trapped us in the house far away from The River.

Cats in their winter lair.

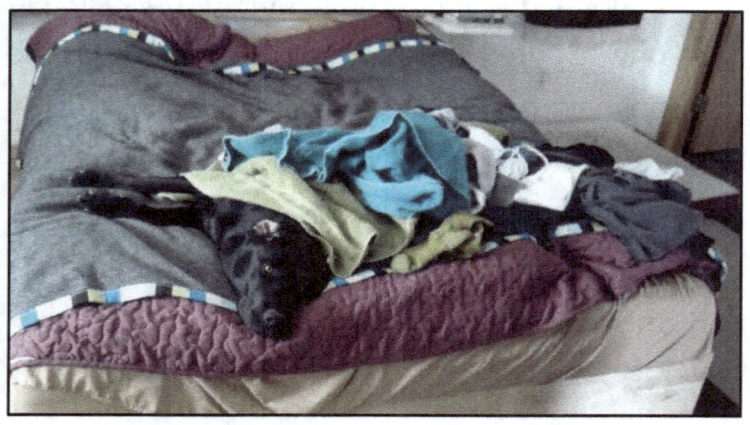

Dog in its winter lair.

We actually own an ice auger and two short ice-fishing poles. One not-very-realistic plan had been brewing in our heads for a couple of years about going ice-fishing, which we simply never committed to and from time to time we spoke with renewed earnest to spend a frozen day out on a lake somewhere fishing through a hole. Our ice gear, though, waited in the shed for that fantasy day. We were too chicken to set the fantasy into motion.

One restless night, we lay on our pillows wondering what the next day would bring to us. Clouds and wind? Snow? Sunny morning? We made sleepy plans to go ice fishing on Skagway Reservoir near Victor in the morning. We planned where on that lake we would drill the holes and Doug told me how we would catch fish by "*jigging*". He told me we could keep our fish (which I am always asking to do) as if we already had them in hand.

"*It'll be OK to keep them,*" Doug said, "*because they're stockers.*" Meaning that the lake is stocked with rainbows. They aren't wild trout. So we won't be removing reproducing fish from the habitat. The stocked trout at Skagway are all of uniform size and girth – and they are dumb. They'll eat crackers right out of your hand in the summer.

That night, I dreamt about trout fishing as I usually do. I was casting to plainly visible fish. I saw the river clearly in my dream: the banks, the sky, the riffles and pools. In this dream, I tried different flies and suddenly foul-hooked a *rubber dog*. It was a species of underwater Labrador dog with gray, smooth skin like a shark (and had four legs). Its mouth did not have teeth. Instead, it had rubber lips like a window squeegee for grabbing trout. This rubber dog had been eating great orange trout underwater in the river like a seal when I foul-hooked it. The rubber Labrador was pleased with itself for having caught so many trout, though it was a little distressed over being hooked by me.

The trout in my dream were visible to me under the water – they were bright orange like goldfish and big as house cats. The fish were feeding in schools in the shallows between the main current and the bank. In my dream, Doug and I figured they must be spawning. Doug scooped one up carefully in his arms and cradled it. Then, he set it down in the water again.

I couldn't figure out if the rubber underwater dog-animal was related to seals or not, but in consideration that seals are, in reality, distantly related to dogs I was satisfied in my dream that the rubber dog really existed. Then, I took the hook out if its side, as I would to a regular foul-hooked fish careful not to harm its unusual rubber skin, and freed it. I didn't catch any fish in my dream but Doug did by the armload of orange trout.

When we woke in the morning, there was a copy of Ed Dentry's book, "*Blue Ribbon Rivers of the Rockies*" lying on the bed between our heads. Doug must have been reading while I slept.

"*I'd rather be on the Kootenai or the Green River than anywhere else in the world today,*" I said to Doug for my first words of the morning.

"*Yeah,*" he answered sleepily, "*Long time no see the BigHorn, either.*"

Thoughts of Montana must be in my cookie jar because when I dig deep for Christmas cookies I get a strong memory of the Yellowstone River below Chico Hot Springs and the colorful cobbles there. These river memories made me decide to send a scanned photo of Texas Hole on New Mexico's San Juan River to Karen Rae Christopherson for her two websites, coloradofishing.net and wyomingfishing.net. It's a unique photo in that there isn't one person in sight on this legendary stretch of river, whereas that venue is usually shoulder to shoulder with anglers.

Texas Hole on the San Juan River, New Mexico – no one in sight.

Why no one fishing on the San Juan in that photo? It was October during off-season between summer and the winter holidays- it was Halloween in that photo, actually. Fortunately for us, no one was there that weekend. The New Mexico Department of Wildlife had just released 125,000 steel-bows below the reservoir. In addition to catching about 100 fish apiece of these whirlers-disease-resistant hybrids, we also caught enormous rainbow and brown trout. It took us six hours to float-fish only a quarter of a mile due to all the fishing action. We only stopped fishing because it became night.

A nice steel-bow in the net.

That Halloween trip to Texas Hole was just like my fishing dream except that it was real life. The trout have slick, huge withers which creasing the surface. They feed by sipping along the current's margin between eddy and riffles like gray whales slowly breaching. I've never seen such large fish in my life as I did on the San Juan below Navajo dam. When we were there, I saw a great tail fin about the size of a large putty spatula cutting the surface as the trout submerged to get away from me.

With my scanned picture sent to Karen, my summer fishing memories filled my winter-trodden day.

One summer day, Doug and I were forced to stop fishing because the planet Earth had rotated us out of the sun's reach for the afternoon and the day's light was gone. I was absentmindedly casting my last attempt to wrangle a specific trout in a long riffle below the "Miracle Pool" on the South Platte's Miracle Mile below Spinney Reservoir near the bridge. When I saw a dorsal fin breach the surface in front of me I realized the monstrous proportion of that hidden fish. I got out of the water and left him for another day.

A lovely trout splashing on the San Juan.

In reality, the winter sun started to come out though the day was half gone by then. In the meanwhile, for lack of ice-fishing, we had rearranged the fly-tying area in the living room, organized our Christmas-gift tackle boxes for the youngsters in the family, and designed a larger rod and gear storage rack area in the back room. It was now almost time for the last Bronco's game of the season to come on television as well. We wasted another day without trying out ice fishing.

'Hmmm – that's another fishing memory as well,' I thought as I remembered watching a football game in Victor, Idaho while waiting for Doug's friend, professional fly fishing guide Kim Keeley, to return to her house so we could get information from her about floating the Snake River. That day, the Broncos lost. They lost again this day as well. *Should have gone ice fishing!*

'Maybe we'll get out to Skagway by New Year's day,' I thought. There was nothing to do but review photos of fish and rivers while it was miserably outside. I turned a page in the photo album.

'Oh – there's that lovely rise on the San Juan of that one particularly nice Brown trout.'

A rising trout on the San Juan River below Texas Hole at Navajo Dam, New Mexico.

And so it goes, winter fish dreams, summer fish memories as so on.... waiting until next season.

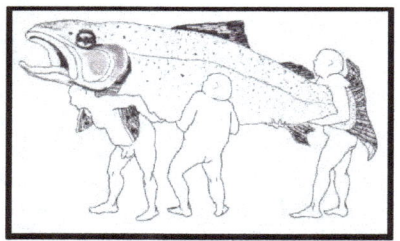

9. DKNY on the Colorado (by Michele White "Murray")

"The Most Famous River Dress of All Time"

I don't want to have to explain in detail why sometimes people (men and women both) might wear a pink neoprene dress on the river in the first place. Suffice it to say; sometimes people wear dresses on the river. More commonly for men, there may be a pair of skorts or painted toenails but a dress is not by any means out of the question. In my experience, a river dress is more comfortable than shorts, easier to take a quick potty, and easier to yank off (should you need to yank your clothes off quickly). River dresses (and skorts) are cool in more ways than one. The dress in question, though, was special: it was a signed exclusive line of Donna Karan New York – a DKNY original – with perhaps as much value (to some) as a signed lithograph by Andy Warhol.

Prudence gave it to me. We were in the habit of trading precious items in exchange for coveted things that each other flaunted in personal possession. Prudence was after my Aunt Charlotte's pink Christian Dior silk and lace bathrobe and I wouldn't give it to her despite my family suggesting that my abode (a 16-foot wide single trailer with 30-year old orange shag carpet and 4 dogs and cats at 10,000 feet elevation in the mountains) was not what Charlotte had in mind when she left her expensive wardrobe to me in her will. Prudence thought the chic robe fit more to her lifestyle than to mine. She lived in a renovated Victorian style home with antique woodwork and stained glass windows in Cripple Creek, Colorado at 9,500 elevation.

I argued. She insisted. I held onto my robe. She asked to "borrow" it though I realized once out of my trailer, I would likely never see it again. I relented and the luscious robe moved to Cripple Creek.

Prudence was once a wealthy aristocrat who lived in Aspen and Durango, Colorado and was a member of a private country club in Denver. She had a long and complex life, but her once high and grand lifestyle is probably where she acquired her taste for style and knew things about labels and brand names. No one knew whereby I acquired my sense of sophistication and fewer knew I even HAVE a sense of sophistication. Prudence knew. She also knew it would take something really special to appease me.

Prudence had in her secret stash of wardrobe, a signed exclusive DKNY but it was not something she would ever wear. It was a bit too gauche for her – being a hot pink, heavy-gauge neoprene, body-forming, party dress. The cut plunged vastly down front-side to expose (and squish) the bosom into shape and the torso snuggly tapered a thin stem-of-a-waist before poofing out into a ballerina-flared skirt with ample flutes and waves about the mid-thigh. Anyone who zipped it on was instantly shaped by thick, pink rubber into this Barbie-form with a cleavage, whether or not they had Barbie-body. It was a perfect swap.

Author in her DKNY neoprene dress.

My DKNY dress debut was to be the weekend of Memorial Day on the Colorado River. The Fezziwigs were bringing a prestigious guest: the daughter of the Vice Chancellor of Germany to the river for her first time. They had been screened by secret police types and the responsibility of her American welfare while on vacation fell into their manicured laps. They invited a careful list of select friends to camp and run the river sans kookiness, on best behavior, no big drunks, keep your clothes on and watch your mouth. I'm not sure if I was invited directly or how I actually ended up in their camp.... But, I had the dress.

We all ran the river together form Pump House to Radium, me at the helm of our own craft wearing my DKNY ("Where'd she get that dress?" I heard them ask. "It's a DKNY original - signed," someone would answer.) My cleavage was bulging. My shoulders hailed the oars. I rowed like a sailor in drag. When my bun rowed, I danced on the bow with agility in my ballet attire and then dove head first into the river for all to see (it was neoprene after all). The young German V.I.P. was never all that close to me, physically, on any occasion because she was in a separate boat but at the Radium Hot Springs (you can land alongside these hot springs directly from the river) we found ourselves seated next to each other and so I felt a compulsory need to make her feel at home by speaking her native tongue:

"Mein GOTT in HIMMEL!!!" I exclaimed. "Wie geht es Ihnen mit dem auto?" (What's up with your car, babe?) "I weiss nicht was soll es bedueten dass ich so traurig bin," (I don't know what is the reason it might be that I am so sad,) - this being a demonstration of knowledge of the High Deutsch arts sure to lighten her heart and make her feel relaxed.

She was maybe, GOB-SMACKED as were her chaperones and I am certain other persons were likely blown away that I am such a polyglot. Who could have known? My sister told me later that they were mortified at me, thought I was blabbering some made-up garble to make fun of the guest's heritage. The German girl (woman, really - a teenager) broke out in a loud belly laugh and blinked back tears before she could answer me (in perfect English) an astonished thank you.

The actual reason I do not wear my dress quite so often anymore is not because of what I hear the hearsay says (that I fell on rocks in a drunken stupor and bled my scabby knees on it, or that the body-forming rubber permanently creased my upper torso, or that the skirt is too short to hide the immensity of my now 50-year old thighs) – none of which is true nor a factor in why I don't wear my DKNY anymore. The real reason I don't wear it anymore is that I haven't been invited to a river running with guests of quite the same caliber. That's all. I am saving it for other international affairs.

Author on bow and bun on stern of dory.

Heinrich Heine, 1822 (1799-1856)

1. Ich weiß nicht, was soll es bedeuten,
Daß ich so traurig bin,
Ein Märchen aus uralten Zeiten,
Das kommt mir nicht aus dem Sinn.
Die Luft ist kühl und es dunkelt,
Und ruhig fließt der Rhein;
Der Gipfel des Berges funkelt,
Im Abendsonnenschein.

2. Die schönste Jungfrau sitzet
Dort oben wunderbar,
Ihr gold'nes Geschmeide blitzet,
Sie kämmt ihr goldenes Haar,
Sie kämmt es mit goldenem Kamme,
Und singt ein Lied dabei;
Das hat eine wundersame,
Gewalt'ge Melodei.

3. Den Schiffer im kleinen Schiffe,
Ergreift es mit wildem Weh;
Er schaut nicht die Felsenriffe,
Er schaut nur hinauf in die Höh'.
Ich glaube, die Wellen verschlingen
Am Ende Schiffer und Kahn,
Und das hat mit ihrem Singen,
Die Loreley getan.

(translation)
1. I cannot determine the meaning
Of sorrow that fills my breast:
A fable of old, through it streaming,
Allows my mind no rest.
The air is cool in the gloaming
And gently flows the Rhine.
The crest of the mountain is gleaming
In fading rays of sunshine.

2. The loveliest maiden is sitting
Up there, so wondrously fair;
Her golden jewelry is glist'ning;

*She combs her golden hair.
She combs with a gilded comb, preening,
And sings a song, passing time.
It has a most wondrous, appealing
And pow'rful melodic rhyme.*

*3. The boatman aboard his small skiff, -
Enraptured with a wild ache,
Has no eye for the jagged cliff, -
His thoughts on the heights fear forsake.
I think that the waves will devour
Both boat and man, by and by,
And that, with her dulcet-voiced power
Was done by the Loreley.*

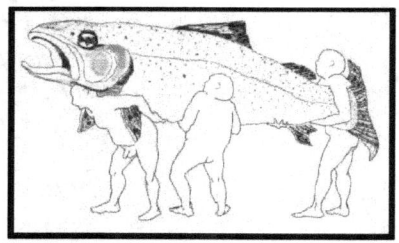

10. Between the Rivers (by Michele White "Murray")

"When a rank situation sweetens up on the road..."

Late into the dark part of night, while on a road trip between the Madison River and the Snake River, our 21-year old motorhome died with our river dory in tow not too far south of Victor, Idaho. We pulled onto the shoulder of either Highway 33 or Highway 22 – not sure if we were in Idaho or Montana, anymore. A person can only view so much of a dark engine that is mounted at chin level with a 5-inch pocket flashlight on the roadside through weary, travel-blurred eyes late at night. We looked anyway. I don't know what my huzbun looks for when an engine dies. The first thing I look for is fire – which would be a significant clue. I saw no smoking wires from my view of the mechanical behemoth from behind his shoulder. Having narrowed the problem down to "a mysterious ailment," I backed off to allow him space to contemplate the sad state of owning this demon of a vehicle. He was in no mood for amateur mechanical advice.

My huzbun's method of analyzing engine problems is predictable and rational, a method proven worthy by the many mechanically deft men in his family. He flung things about and cursed the swindler who sold the thing to him. I stood back and watched this otherwise calm man shake the vehicle about, terrifying our sleepy dogs with cursing – certain words of which, even when muttered under his breath, automatically render the poor, neurotic things to a state of shivering jelly. My method of engine analysis is to start replacing things that I can reach first, such as a broken fuel pump, leaking water pump, plugged fuel filter, lack of oil, dying alternator. I had complete faith in him to isolate the issue at hand by himself with more scientific address. He might jiggle loose a suspicious dangling wire in his tirade that needed to be reattached or something as simple to fix might become apparent. Fortunately, I'd seen a sign for a bar along the highway shortly before the engine began lurching. I had learned from previous engine problems near Craig, Montana that having a cocktail makes this situation lighter to endure.

As I meandered down the highway looking for sign of the bar I had seen, I thought of the day's events. Some mechanical contraption in the engine must have come loose or begun to disintegrate earlier that afternoon when we were bumping down a particularly bad, rutted road in our decrepit jalopy. I had been the one at the wheel and it was my idea to go exploring off the main highway down an unmarked dirt road, in assumption that it might lead us in the vicinity of two little blue spots labeled "*Twin Lakes*" on the Idaho map. These lakes were not listed in the published literature of our traveling library for fly fishing in the region, but I had a vision of discovering them: two beautiful, clear blue remote lakes to be enjoyed by ourselves in solitude for belly-boat fishing.

Shortly after diverging from the main route, the dirt road became rockier and narrower. We were jostled over the washboard surface until our skeletons rearranged at the joints under our skin and our possessions fell from the overhead cupboards in a dust-coated heap on top of the dogs in the middle of the aisle. We noticed at the same time, that there seemed to be more dust inside the motorhome than outside on the road.

'Bun ordered me to stop. An investigation revealed that the backend of the chassis extended beyond the interior floor of the coach making for a gap of about 5 inches to the open road below, which was partially concealed by a few rags stuffed beneath the shag carpet. When the carpet was pulled back and the rags removed, we could see the ground directly beneath us through the gap. That was where the road dust in the vehicle was coming from so intently.

By the time we stopped to investigate this dust phenomenon, we were experiencing a general state of annoyance common to married couples on road trips. I was willing to admit I might be lost and I may have made a bad decision when leaving the main, marked road. In this altered mental state, I attempted to turn the huge rig (motorhome and dory) around by three-point backing and pulling forward in a star-shaped pattern at the intersection of the little road with a cross-cutting access to a pasture. As a result, I succeeded in wedging our long rig into a state of 'stuckedness', whereas our vehicle and boat were exactly jack-knifed between the narrow margins of the bounding ditches with no room to go either forward or backward. (This is an extreme state of parking, for which I have a particular talent.)

Aware of my recent shortcomings as a navigator, I requested Doug to please take over the helm as I had done as much as I desired to do. He removed his clenched knuckles from his forelock, moved to the driver's seat, and engaged the motorhome engine to scream with power as he rammed the gears into and out of a selection of ratios both forward and backwards to spur the machine down into and up out of the weed-filled ditch in front of us, nearly toppling us over on our side. After the swinging contents of our possessions fell from ajar the overhead compartments and the dust cloud inside the cab began to settle, I could see through our windshield that we were now facing the direction where we had come from.

Doug got out of the driver's seat with the vehicle still running and stuffed newspapers into the gap between the chassis and the floor. Then, he drove us like a madman back to the main road. Probably, that venture is what jostled something in the motorhome's engine to a state of death.

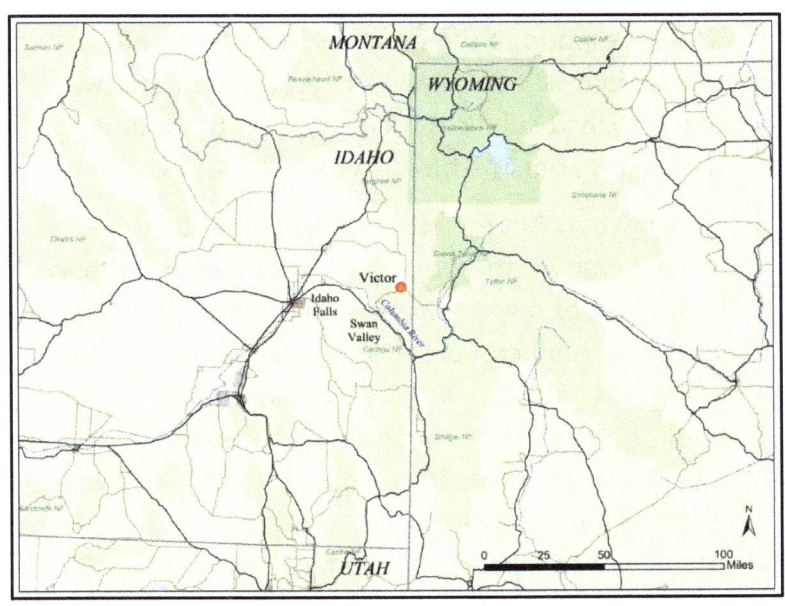

Location of Victor, Idaho.

Now, in the middle of the same day's night, Doug seemed surprised as I wandered away from him that I didn't want to witness another fit. I thought for 3 seconds about staying with him – to insure him all would turn out fine in the morning. We could have a night cap and commiserate this event together, like one of those "through thick and thin" sort of things you hear so much about at weddings. He is always so patient with me. However, I remembered some vague atrocity committed by some vague boyfriend in the past – a memory of being victimized by every single man I have ever met in my entire life or something like that – and decided I should respond to the distinct voice of a cocktail calling to me from what looked like might be a bar down the highway, across a field. I left Doug with the dogs in the stink of his anger faithful he would fix the engine.

They have a different sense of humor up there in Idaho. On my walk to the bar, I had to cut across a moonlit, frosty field of tall, dry autumn grass, which obscured a young woman crouching in a pink bathrobe. I walked nearly on top of her. She was not only wearing a bathrobe, but she also wore black, webbed curlers in her hair. Really. She seemed normal, even attractive: blonde, slim and young. By the time I stumbled upon her in the dark, we were already face to face. I looked directly into her face and saw that maybe it was only the circumstance that was weird looking, not actually the woman herself. She didn't have a crazy look in her eye.

Immediately, she began to explain that she was stalking her brother who was drinking at my point of destination. She asked me to check on his status for her because their ol' Auntie had died that afternoon and this worthless brother was no good for having gone hunting instead of hanging out with the family and then he went bar-hopping when the family was in need of him for solace. Seemed logical to me. Nothing weird about a sister lurking in the field, in lieu of her ol' Auntie dying. If I had funeral arrangements to attend in the morning, I might need to stand in curlers out in a field in the middle of the night, too. I left her in the weeds and continued my mission with newly expanded purpose.

The bar looked closed – no lights visible on the outside. A thin, hollow-core kind of door – the type that might be used for a bathroom door in a trailer – provided the front entrance. This entrance was also obscured by a facade of pseudo hunting lodge ornamentation (split logs) that barely distinguished the building from any of the other half-fallen, old mechanics' outbuildings and junk collections along the highway. I opened the door and entered into a dimly lit nest of camouflaged, drinking men, a few of whom had rifles propped near them.

I was surprised that the bar was so dark but saw there was a dance floor – which is a sign of sociable people that dance with women one would assume. Then, I noticed that there were also some women seated in the bar of the hard-life but still-alive variety of backwoods,

Idaho women. That was another good sign– this being a woman-drinking tolerant bar rather than a gentleman only establishment.

A girl has to do what a girl has to do under these circumstances. The local patrons were all staring at me as if the movie, 'Deliverance,' was a love story. So, I greeted them all as a group slightly formally and launched into a bar joke. '*Did they hear the one about the woman who got lost in Idaho and entered a local bar way out in the middle of nowhere?*'

As my joke goes, a woman gets lost, enters a bar where a local guy befriends her and then fandangles her into jumping out of a window over a cliff because he demonstrates to her how the wind catches him when he jumps out the window and blows him back up on the windowsill. When she tries it, however, she falls. No wind catches her. My joke ends by the bartender in the joke saying to the local guy in the joke, "*You sure are a jerk when you've been drinking, Superman.*" The reaction to my epilogue in the Idaho bar was silence and some blinking red eyes. I ordered an MGD.

I was wondering to myself if maybe my joke was too complicated for that time of night, especially when everyone had been drinking for a few hours already. I could see that the hunters' ears under their blaze-orange baseball caps were smoking as creaky cogs turned in their minds rehashing my joke. Probably, they weren't aware that their eyes were bulging out at me like shocked oysters. I realized then, that some of them were thinking that maybe I was trying to relay a true story – that maybe I really saw some lady jump off a cliff at some other bar in Idaho. I was wondering to myself, how then, I might go about convincing them it was not a true story without coming off as some big fat liar from some big fat city. Unfortunately, not to be condescending, but the biggest thing in some of those heads seemed to be their tongues.

Gradually, a camouflaged large one of them asked me where I came from. I truthfully said, "*Victor*". This produced an element of suspicion amongst the group as I didn't look like nor act like anyone from Victor, Idaho. So, I added, "*Victor, COLORADO*". That had a good effect. I could see he was thinking that if there are two towns named Victor in the United States, then, it's possible we could be related in some way. Kind of like getting each other's mail mixed up at the post office or having one account for two different families named, 'White,' at the video store.

This big hunting-man then spread his large hands on the bar, leaned over me and put on a big, joke-telling face and told his own joke – something about a little bird that found itself buried in a pile of bull poop. Then, another guy put on his big, joke-telling face and told his joke about some other type of situation in a blizzard (the theme being bad things that have happened to people with morals to the stories. The humor was actually quite sophisticated, you see). This was good. I could see I was safe to have a beer now without fear of being expunged by Bambi killers. I was accepted.

At some point, my wonderful huzbun walked in and joined me at the bar. He told me that he wanted to test the alternator. The camouflaged guys overheard him mention the alternator and they stirred in their seats. Something stimulated them about the idea of a mechanical problem waiting down the road in the middle of the night. Their instincts responded to the call of emergency. They knew the routine: stranded on the road, belly up to the vehicle's grill with a flashlight, hovering with greasy sleeves over an evil, crippled engine. Great excuse not to go home quite yet to the little women waiting for them in black, webbed curlers. Every one of the camouflaged men had a pocket full of engine problem opinions based on what their Daddies taught them soon as they were big enough to hand Daddy a Phillips-head screwdriver. As a result, a bunch of the camo-guys surrounded my bun and followed him outside to go look under the hood with a bunch more assorted flashlights.

It was just then, as a few of them were shuffling out the bathroom door that served as the main entrance, that the brother whose sister was stalking him, lost control of his 7 mm hunting rifle and shot a hole in the floor (7-mm bullets are quite large, big as a fat girl's middle finger). He later said he had been fiddling with the safety latch. This action resulted in a slow, ghostlike evacuation of the entire bar, which left me in the position of being this guy's only companion. (Doug, who was already outside, later told me he thought the noise was someone's truck backfiring.) This errant-brother-irresponsible-hunter guy was very enthusiastic about discussing our alternator with me. He wanted to appear to be real helpful (in case I, like everyone else, might think he was an idiot, I suppose). I suggested he also go outside and join the rest of the gang looking at the engine, as this was men's business. I certainly didn't want him to join me. He left obediently.

Local bartender not so easily won over by stories.

I hailed my neglected beer and focused on loosening up the lone bartender (a woman who was not so easily accepting of my outlandish arrival, because women are warier than men are and because there was a fresh bullet hole in her floor as an indirect result of this unusual night's company). I was trying to amuse her with a slow barrage of elementary school jokes I've collected from various five-year olds I've known, when the same errant-brother-irresponsible-hunter guy returned with my bun in a '70 Chevy pickup (I deduced its year by comparing it to my own '71 at home). His truck had four different colored fenders. No grill. Probably no insurance or license plates for that matter either, let alone seat belts. Certainly no rearview mirror. No more rifle, either. My bun was slightly wobbly and told me that he had been subjected to a little bit of Dickel with the hunter-brother.

Someone had given our battery a jump and the motor home was running in the parking lot with the dory behind it like the Frankenstein Monster arisen from the dead toting a toy choo-choo. (The battery would temporarily hold a charge, but the alternator wouldn't regenerate it, so we couldn't go too far). The hunter-brother directed us in the motor home to about halfway down the bartender's father-in-law's second ex-wife's mile long driveway, next door. Our motor home finally died for good in front of some gutted out jeeps without windshields hidden in the tall weeds. Some of the jeeps were only visible by their "for sale" signs in the driver's seats. I had a vision of our motor home resting there amongst the jeeps, like a freak of nature for a long time.

Then, of course not to be rude, we had to accept an invitation to dinner (1 a.m.) at the hunter-brother's 15-foot, single-wide mobile (not anymore) home. The five of us, (hunter-brother, bun, myself, and our two dogs), had macaroni & cheese – the hunter-brother wouldn't eat white cheese or a cauliflower my mother had given to me a week earlier but the dogs did – and hamburger patties, (which we forgot until a couple of hours later when we discovered them still sitting in the black, cast-iron skillet looking like cold poverty).

I saw things in his bathroom that only stinky ol' bachelor men have in their bathrooms. Unmentionable things. My handsome huzbun was handling the evening's events with pioneer stamina. This unusual side-trip was probably not much different from hanging out with his older brothers who occasionally invited him on wild fishing expeditions, like he was their pet mascot. One comes to learn that these rank sorts of situations sometimes sweeten up if you're open minded enough to enjoy unusual events. Besides, some of the nicest people in the world are stinky 'ol bachelors.

Before long, the hunter-brother showed us his guns. It was around 3 in the morning when our host told us that he was an ex-felon and not allowed to have a gun in his possession. EVER. But he trusted us. He emphasized that point: HE TRUSTED US. (And, we bet he could find us, too – even if it was a decade down the road and we lived in a teepee on the backside of a mountain in Tibet.) He also showed us his beautiful, custom buck-knife collection – gifts from his estranged children – evidence of their love for him. His knife collection was very touching.

When we finally left Jim's house, the new day was dawning. (We picked his name up somewhere between macaroni dinner and the rest of the Dickel.) The whole community had turned out to view the 7 mm hole in the bar room floor. Everybody was eyeing Jim like he had made a poop on the floor or some such nasty thing. But, Jim was happy because he had new friends. Since they were at the bar already, most everyone (not us) had a morning shot and a beer. No one would take our money. Not even the bartender's father-in-law's second ex-wife (Nancy) for camping in her driveway. They closed their eyes, turned their faces away from our money and held their palms up to deflect the dollars. Our money was no good there.

It's important to accept people's generosity and to occasionally allow strangers to help you. That's how trust and brotherhood still manage to hang on in this wacky world. But, in order not to take advantage, I argued I had won money at Bingo in Craig, Montana and waved a wedge of five dollar bills at the bar tab. We had been traveling around errantly fly fishing from the Colorado River to The Great Missouri and all rivers in between, when I needed to access more cash. I withdraw $200 from an ATM machine in Craig, Montana, which only dispensed five dollar bills. When my bun saw the 2-inch slab of five dollar bills that was too thick to fold in half coming out of the machine he exclaimed, "*BINGO*".

Under a hail of good-byes and well-wishes from the crowd and with thanks to each person, we drove away. We felt like relatives visiting from afar. Sometime during the night's escapades, all of us had transformed into some kind of clan from the ancient days. Maybe we were reincarnated. We recognized each other as members of the same Early Holocene tribe who used to live along the banks of the Snake River, thousands of years ago.

The friendly Idaho folk watched us until we drove out of sight. I'm sure they were expecting to witness the next break down – perhaps the axle falling off or the engine finally igniting. In fact, the morning light had revealed a suspicious wire dangling from the alternator. When reattached (and recharged) the engine ran fine (for a fume-generating, noisy, tortoise-paced engine) all the way back to Victor, Colorado with a few more stops along and between other rivers.

The 22-year old demon.

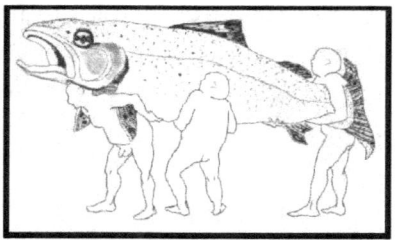

11. Binkler's Butterball (by Michele White "Murray")

"Bringing the Love-Stroke to the Mountains."

There is a tribe of underfed, (and probably intoxicated), good-humored River People who have been camping together along the banks of the Colorado River between the frothy throat of Gore Canyon's sluice-box below Kremmling and its eventual confluence with the Eagle River above Glenwood Canyon for tens of thousands of years. This ancient tribe evolved over time into a unique family, as they became isolated from their mainstream origins. Their culture encompassed a microcosm within a unique ecological niche of Mountain and River below the angular unconformity of yellow and red sedimentary rocks of the "State Bridge Formation," where it juts into the basaltic base of mystical Mount Yarmony, spiritual redoubt of Ute Indian Chiefs.

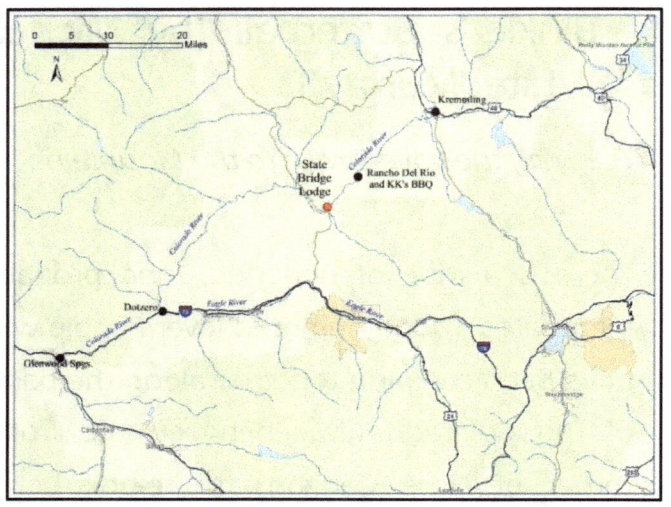

Location of State Bridge Lodge, Colorado.

State Bridge Lodge (1994) and the geological structure: "State Bridge Angular Unconformity" contact.

In the last hundred years, this tribe has shared the banks with an influx of newcomers, "River-Virgins", toting a variety of luggage for portage, which originally included beaver pelts, industrial novelties such as apple-corers and automated washing machines, railroad timbers, and other stuff desired by turn-of-the-century society. On summer weekends, the tribe portages apparati for kayaking, fly fishing, rafting and other wet hullabalooing. One weekend last century, a River-Virgin named Cory Binkler arrived at the undulating lip of the Colorado River with a frozen turkey. Cory was a plasma-physicist from Seattle, Washington; he was known for his charisma.

Cory had arrived at a place on The River referred to in his directions as "Uncle Charlie's Blue-Tarp City on the banks of the Colorado across the river from State Bridge Lodge," was set up over a circle of tents and backpacks. He reread the handwritten invitation from his childhood friend, Katie, who was still floating on The River, slowly float-fishing in a dory between Rancho del Rio and Catamount. Uncle Charlie—a zesty, cantankerous river guide with a wild, white pony tail under a very beat-up Stetson cowboy hat—had constructed the enormous, crazily dipping canopy out of a 30' by 30' blue-tarp (as only an ex-denizen of the Vietnam jungle can).

Uncle Charlie and author.

The blue plastic tarp covered a large area in a campground across The River from State Bridge Lodge, which is an outdoor music venue. Charlie intended Blue-Tarp City as an open stay-over destination for the tribe and people who drove up from Denver to hear the band. The River People knew one only needed to float down the river casually and, at the end of the day, watch for an enormous blue tarp. They knew All People were welcome. That's why Katie invited Cory Binkler to meet her there on his long overdue vacation to Colorado.

Uncle Charlie's "Blue Tarp City".

For some reason, Uncle Charlie was fascinated with Cory Binkler from the get go. Maybe it was the plasma physics, maybe it was Cory's ponytail, but Charlie's fascination with Cory may have been due to the frozen turkey. Cory Binkler had chauffeured a 24-pound frozen bird from his apartment in Seattle to The River in Colorado. Charlie was astounded by the bird as well as by Cory's initial request:

"Does anyone have a large grill?"

Cory overestimated the quality of the facilities. He asked kayakers, rafters, and residents of a teepee if anyone had a large grill or other sort of sophisticated cooking device. He was offered a tripod over a stone ring. Charlie balanced the bird atop a conspicuous boulder like an unidentified corpse at the morgue for all to see and inspect.

Cory wasn't totally unprepared. He had brought necessary items: a sleeping bag, sunglasses, oven-mitts, a cooking thermometer, ballpoint pens, charcoal briquettes, and apple-wood branches, all of which formed a nest of debris in the backseat of his car. No grill, though. "Bird-zilla" had traveled all the way from the Great Woods of the Northwest in a large, "thermally-dynamic," battery-dependent cooler in the trunk of his car only to be stared at by all in its solidified state. Cory went about creating a space for himself and looking after his personal hygiene, un-baffled.

Later in the evening awaiting Katie's arrival from The River, Cory borrowed Charlie's axe — a professional, logger-sized weapon nearly as big as himself. He staggered backwards under the weight, then muscled it forward in an alarming dive at what everyone assumed to be the ice-ball of a bird in order to downsize it into reasonable proportions. However, Cory was only hacking his apple-wood branches into chips. Some of the River People coached him how to avoid chopping his feet off. By the time Katie arrived, he had reduced not only his little branches to shredded slivers, but also one great log that couldn't get away.

"What?" Katie asked Charlie. "He brought a frozen turkey?" She was obviously pleased to see Cory in camp and amazed to see him all grimy and sweaty. But she also seemed a little embarrassed by her friend's bulging bundle of bird on display by the campfire.

"What are you going to do with it?" she asked.

"I didn't know what I should bring. You said there were probably going to be lots of people. I just brought this turkey. I have a special recipe. Can you please help me find an oven or a large grill tomorrow? It's really important. If I don't cook it within a certain amount of time, it won't work."

"We'll see." Katie answered with sincere doubt.

In the morning, the River People had shuttled their crafts upriver to Rancho Del Rio. The plan for the day was to float back to State Bridge Lodge in time for the music and campout at Blue-Tarp City. A soiree of native-looking types (for Gilligan's Island, maybe) with ragamuffin beaded hair twitches, leather-thong necklaces, Patagonia river shorts and Chaco sandals, were seated at KK's BBQ stand at Rancho drinking beer. It was 9 o'clock in the morning and they were waiting for their river-guests to arrive. KK's BBQ is strategically located in the middle of Rancho's grounds—one has to drive slowly around her stand and be examined by the local professionals before reaching the parking area. By the time the tourists have unloaded, smeared themselves with sun-block, packed purses and pockets to be left behind with all their valuable possessions with their outfitters (and kissed life-as-they-know-it good-bye), the local river runners are fairly geared up.

The motley river crew.

Cory was becoming frantic. He had to GET THE BIG BALD BIRD A-COOKIN' by a certain time or else it would not get done. He stressed over this matter even before Katie was awake. By the time they arrived at Rancho, Cory had concocted a backup plan. He immersed the big frozen bird in Charlie's five-gallon plastic bailing bucket, where it soaked in brine laced with the apple-wood chips. The resourceful cook then stowed it in Katie's dory to be shuttled up to Rancho.

When they arrived, Cory hauled the troublesome carcass to KK—a woman who seemed to be the hub of the Universe. He hoped she might let him use part of her huge grill for the next five hours. Though she is one of the most gracious hosts to be found in three counties, Cory had no idea he was dealing with the most focused and intense Bar-B-Q woman on this planet. KK utilizes every inch of her grill to cook up piles of ribs, chicken, brats, burgers, and wieners for the hungry souls of the district.

KK's BBQ – Center of the Known Universe, at Rancho Del Rio.

Katie's tolerance evaporated when Cory attempted to return the rejected bird to her dory. The River was high and she wanted to fish. It would take a strong oarsman to row three people, two fat dogs, and a 24-pound suckling-sized turkey in a bucket of brine against the current in order to cast into trout lairs without being hurried.

Katie thought she might release the turkey into the river to have it bob through eddies and rapids like flotsam. A vision of it washing up at the campsite all bloated and FOUL put her off this plan. (Also, river regulations forbid the dumping of solid waste into the stream.) Fortunately for Cory, whose composure was cracking, Charlie responded. He put the bucket of frozen-bird-and-brine in the storage of his raft.

Katie met one of her regular fishing pals at KK's BBQ stand. They put Cory and two dogs in the stern of the dory, and then pushed off. Charlie loaded four guests and THE BIG DEAD BIRD into his raft. Both boats were full of beer and food in coolers, too. Charlie knew Katie would be rowing against the current to slow her boat and hover at nice, fishy holes, so he planned to take his people on land expeditions in the meantime. He had places where he tied up his raft for hiking up to Ute Indian ruins, old eagle-traps, fur trappers' cabins and even dinosaur tracks. Katie would do nothing but fish the entire day. She intended to use Cory as her slave at the oars.

Shortly after the current sucked the bow of the dory downstream into a seam of faster moving water, Cory began fiddling and fussing with a piece of twine he had produced from his shirt pocket. He had put this string in a little plastic bag—the kind that zips. In an instant, he fashioned hand-made "river-gear" for attaching his glasses and hat to a buttonhole on his shirt. Katie wasn't sure if she should be amazed or annoyed with him.

Cory noticed her inspecting gaze. "Remember that time I almost lost my hat in the wind?" he asked her. "Now, I don't have to worry about losing either my hat or my glasses!" He was clearly pleased with his systematic approach.

"Here, Cory. Watch how I hug the bank and keep the boat parallel to the shoreline. Think you can do this?" Katie asked.

Her enlisted man rowed most of the day—certainly through all the big, slow "lakes" where the river widened and offered little current for assistance. It's not an easy job to scoot around in a lake when the water is "greasy" either, as was the case in many of these great pools. "Greasy" water occurs where the current is upwelling from below to the surface and sucking back down again in plumes. There is no orientation or direction to the current, though it can produce a deceitful, strong undertow which can yank an oar right out of the helmsman's hands. The surface has a glossy, wrinkled texture that literally looks greasy.

The wind also had picked up making it more difficult to keep the dory in a straight line.

Cory began raising his arched body into the air with his pelvis jutted forward and leaned back on the oars as they slowly dipped and descended into the current.

"What are you doing, Cory?" Katie asked." You're scaring me."

"It's the 'love-stroke', Momma! I'm applying the weight of my body to the torque-force of these levers and converting potential energy into kinetic energy, which requires much less muscle-energy in addressing the inertia of this ship."

Katie tried hard to freeze her smile. This odd man moved her heart as surely as he moved the dory. The "Charm of Cory" was upon her. She remembered why she loved him despite the distance and time that separated their lives. She never intended to let the years slip by—it just happened. Now, they were both in their thirties and neither had ever been married though both had been close (not to each other). Whenever she met him, Cory opened her heart and filled it with wonderful, life-enriching sustenance. He was one of her most favorite people in the world. Once, Cory had commenced a self-imposed moratorium on visiting or even contacting her for nearly five years. She felt as if a significant beacon on which she had come to rely for grounding and centering in her chaotic life had been extinguished. (They never talked about the reason why—she just assumed she had been an asshole.) A world without Cory was a world with a big, cold hole in it. Katie wondered if he knew how she felt about him, if he knew how valuable he was to her. But she never asked.

"Those 'levers' are called 'oars.' Can you slow us down a bit, Mr. Love-Stroke?" she responded.

When they came to the big, faster water either Katie or her fellow angler took over the oars. At those times, Cory delighted in hanging one hand over the gunnels while holding onto a beer with the other. He laughed at the mist of white-capped rapids as they were decapitated by the chine of the dory's hull and sprayed his face. Otherwise, Cory rowed Katie's and her buddy's butt and the turkey and dogs all the way downriver against the wind and with growing prowess at the sticks.

Cory was quickly becoming comfortable with his new role. He spoke and joked in the voice of a pirate. The fishing duo tried not to laugh at everything he said. He was visibly enjoying torturing his captives with both his silly comedy routine and with physical experiments of dexterity at the oars. He quickly realized he could use eddies to return upstream to offer fish-filled riffles to his "shipmates" again and again. No one was thinking about cooking the damn bird anymore. Katie wondered if she could infiltrate a clan of Cory's friends and colleagues as easily as he adapted to the creed of her unsophisticated friends. She knew he envied her lifestyle (everyone in the city did), but she didn't know if he sensed how much she admired him, that she believed him to be the deeper, more developed person.

"Cory, I'll ask the owners at State Bridge if I can use one of the ovens in their restaurant. They're my friends." But it didn't look like Cory was worried about his bird Buddha anymore. One fine day on The River had transformed him into River Man. He was truly content just rowing them all about, in and out of eddies, slowing only for suspected trout hideouts. He held the dory right on line with the drift—as if he had been doing it all is life.

"Oh, that would be perfect, Katie."

Unfortunately, State Bridge Lodge had a large wedding reception going and the kitchen was rock—n'—rolling with swinging cooks and waitresses who seemed as happy to be working as the guests were to be dancing. Charlie and the other guides had joined their guests who were already in a high state of alcohol-induced entropy and no longer River-Virgins. Fortunately for Cory, the genuinely friendly bartender (as ALL the bartenders at State Bridge ALWAYS are) offered a two-legged Weber grill without lid or grate from his cabin. It was a true roadside grill—found by the side of the highway. Uncle Charlie briefly left his devoted entourage to devise a third—and much needed—leg from a prolific junk pile behind the lodge. Further rousting in the garbage produced a refrigerator shelf, which, after Charlie bent the corners, made for a grate. Now, the plasma physicist was ready to commence the brawn work.

Cory fashioned a chimney from two economy-size coffee cans. He perforated and filled them with charcoal. Katie was intrigued to observe that stacked vertically inside this vented reactor briquettes burned much more efficiently. Next, Cory made Katie's fishing lackey hold three long sheets of aluminum foil at arms' length as he rolled a seam between them and constructed a large astrodome. The engineer-chef then placed his brine-soaked apple-wood chips on the grill as a bed for one magnificently huge turkey—now flabby and waving its arms about like a needy chimpanzee. When the wood-chips began to smolder he nestled Big Bird in them and covered her nudity with the foil dome. The gone-camping-and-floating turkey was now beginning to resemble dinner. The scent of Thanksgivings hung in the air but this congregation of scantily clad, drunken River People reminded Katie more of a bacchanal.

The motley crew danced and carried-on to a live band at the lodge for five hours straight while Cory repeatedly stuck his thermometer in the chest cavity of the turkey until it reached a critical temperature. When the bird's magical transition had satisfied the scientist, he presented the amazing, golden bird to the crowd with oven-mitts and the flourish of a doctor delivering a newborn to its mother. The lodge owners laid out buns, forks, plates and napkins. Everyone ordered side dishes of potatoes and other tasty morsels from the kitchen and feasted on the moist, smoked turkey as if they had never eaten one before. In the morning, there were even leftovers for next day's regatta.

After Cory left The River to return to his Seattle life as one of Boeing's Project Directors or something to that effect,

Katie learned of his Internet Website for smoking turkeys. ("How do you get one into a pipe?" was her initial reaction.) One recipe featured an "Expedition-worthy Tur-Duck-Hen," a Turkey-stuffed-with-duck-stuffed-with-chicken like Russian dolls. She didn't expect to see Cory again for a while—probably a long while. That's just the way it has always been between them. Katie, however, knew she wouldn't be surprised if one day she came floating around a bend and saw Cory at the "levers" of another dory, demonstrating the "love-stroke" to a duo of fly-fishermen trying to hide their mirth from this odd bird.

Denizens of the Colorado River livin' in a teepee.

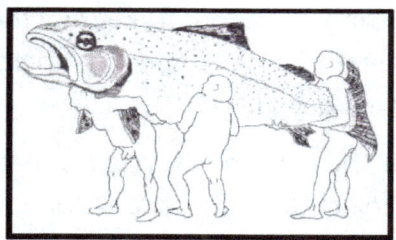

12. Floating the Beaverhead in a Wooden Tub (by Michele White "Murray")

"A fishing adventure in western Montana"

Russell Quimbley lives in Ramsay, Montana near Butte, as do other guys who like to fish the many tributaries and headwaters of the Clark Fork and Jefferson Rivers. Years ago, he introduced us to the Beaverhead Fork of the Jefferson River by floating us merrily-life-is-but-a-dream-style in a smelly old rubber raft. Since then, he bought an old boat, a hand-hewn wooden dory, the 'Rub-a-Dub-Tub'. At first glance, 'The Tub' looks like a nicely crafted McKenzie-style dory, though it's not as streamlined. Its sides are 3 feet high, making for significant drag in even a light breeze. If it's windy, he has to row like a slave at sea to move downstream. The 'Tub' was probably the product of someone's tinkering Dad, birthed in a home garage with birdfeeders and whirly-gigs. It is, however, unexpectedly stalwart.

Though the clarity of the Beaverhead can be cloudy above its confluence with the Big Hole (the combination of which form the Jefferson River), its murky eddies contain abundant, large Brown trout with hooked snouts and spikey teeth. Capturing these big animals is the main purpose of floating this upper part of the river, as most people fish the lower section where the water is clear and the trout, though smaller, are more abundant. Russell Quimbley likes to float-fish from above the confluence to five miles below their united lineage using crimped barbs for catch and release purposes. He is a purist fisherman in that respect.

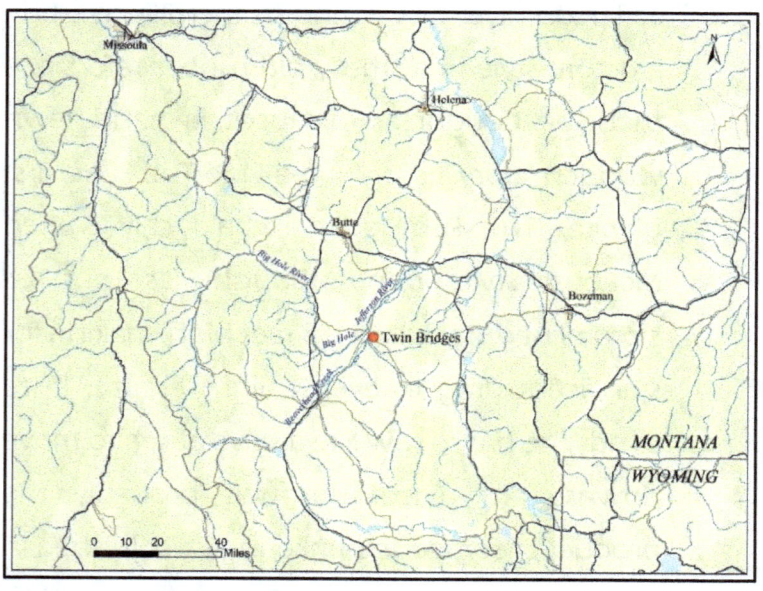

Twin Bridges on the Beaverhead Creek above the Big Hole River.

Russell puts The Tub in at Twin Bridges Community Park and takes out on BLM property above Silver Star. This stretch of the Jefferson is not very technical to navigate except for a rare submerged Cottonwood tree after a heavy rainstorm. The first couple of miles are not very scenic unless you appreciate cement blocks and aggregate concretions. The Beaverhead is drawn upon heavily for agricultural purposes and along this stretch is confined like an irrigation canal between artificial banks with an occasional iron Re-bar sticking out. Above the confluence with the Big Hole, the Beaverhead slips by the backyards of houses providing a tour of laundry safari. One can hear kids barking and dogs giggling. The river's character changes near the confluence to a braided-meander with shallow sandbars and abundant islands through an expanse of over-bank flood plains, heavily treed with cottonwoods and willow bushes sheltering wildlife, such as deer, fox, heron and raccoon. The main channel is consistently deep through this flood plain and friendly to dory expeditions.

The lack of shuttles requires Russell, (who is a natural manager), to coordinate with his friends (most of whom are his employees) to retrieve the boat at the end of the day. Usually, Russell will extend a general invitation to his employee / buddies hoping someone will turn up. Once, though, a group of seven big guys with names like, "Tank" and "Bubby", arrived at the park with fishing gear, lunches and 4 cases of the most economical, canned beer – all hoping to go float-fishing.

As a leader of men, Russell is known for assessing tricky situations and providing a practical solution. He rolled a fat cigar around on his jaw while he planned how to handle this situation.

Wooden Tub and her crew.

Russell is confident and competent - a good combination for a river skipper. On that morning, Russell Quimbley eyeballed the crew and their mass of stowage, rolled his cigar from one corner of his mouth to the other. Then, he provided this plan: one guy standing with two guys sitting behind him in the front end, one oarsman in the middle, two guys sitting and one guy standing in the back. They'd have to stack the cases of beer, (sooner than later, they wouldn't have to worry about that commodity anymore.)

Everyone put this proposal into effect. No one wanted to be left behind confined like an exile to fish from the banks of the community park only to return home without having floated on the river at all. When they disembarked, the tall sides of The Tub were submerged to within 3 inches of the gunnels. She groaned a little, too, bobbing down-stream.

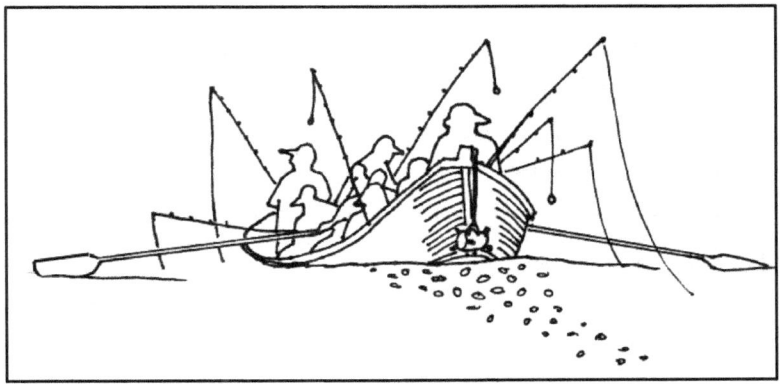

A full load from gunnel to gunnel.

Casting aboard The Tub was executed in ranks three at a time. Some of the men were satisfied to troll their rigged line behind the brave wooden boat or flick their lure alongside and under the keel for those Navy Seal type of trout. Some used worms or Powerbait. All in all, fish were going to be caught. Everyone was happy to be included and looked forward to a fine day on the river. Their thoughts were far from tasks of automotive maintenance, gutter repair, manure spreading, and a bazillion other weekend chores now abandoned at home.

Fortunately for the crew, Russell suggested everyone crimp their barbs for the sake of human eyes and skin. Russell Quimbley usually released trout for good sportsmanship but his crew only released the smaller ones – and their method was primitive. They hugged the flapping critter to their chest to remove the hook. Then, dropped the freed fish like a discarded sock over the side. Despite these terrible releases the small fish seemed to swim away unharmed. The larger more horrible trout were kept in the bilge at their feet to be made into dinner when they got home.

Bubba and his trout.

The Tub wobbled along. The worried oarsman could hardly direct the submerged belly of the engorged boat down the channel. As they lumbered slowly, the gunnels dipped slightly from side to side. The men were careful to hold their positions and use their weight to keep the rim above water. The first two miles of the Beaverhead, being confined by banks of cement, run deep and require less negotiation from the oarsman. Occasionally, though, the sound of flat-hull scraping over some hidden threat resulted in momentary silence and big eyes from the crew. But, the reliant Tub drifted on.

Unfortunately for the underwater fauna, the arrival of this nearly submerged vessel hailed what seemed to a trout to be an interesting clutter of shimmering things to eat, similar to a school of minnows or some underwater hatch of nymphs accompanying an errant manatee. So, it was that Russell Quimbley's crew managed to accumulate a keel-load of Brown trout with a rare Rainbow and even one tenacious crawdad, clinging and cursing in crustacean-dialect to the shredded neck of a worm. Some of the fish were so large they would have impressed a commercial tuna hunter (if a tuna hunter were to be found). These especially large animals added weight to The Tub's cargo.

About mid-morning, the dory was approaching the confluence. Tank had been dragging the anchor behind them by a rope for a slowing effect with his fishing line draped over the stern. The Tub entered an eddy and began to slowly spin uncontained by Bubby, the oarsman. Tank's fishing line became entangled with the anchor line and he made verbal hoopla over the mess blaming Bubby for his lack of prowess at the oars. While peace was disrupted, Chuck (sitting next to Tank) chomped Tank's line off with his teeth and then nursed his own line over the stern. That action enraged Tank and more words flew. Admonished, Chuck reeled his line in, but it also became entangled with the anchor line.

Of course, when Tank pulled the anchor line up to retrieve his lure he gave Chuck's line a similar liberating chomp. Chuck reacted with righteous wrath as the intensity of the spat inched up a notch. Now, the rest of the crew focused with amusement. When Tank pulled the anchor clear of the water, they saw an enormous, flopping Brown trout dangling from the anchor with a lure stuck to its snout. Everyone was just amazed. Chuck immediately claimed the fish to be caught on his tangled line that Tank bit off. Tank argued that the fish was hooked on his tangled line that Chuck bit off - and he argued further that he was the one who had been operating the anchor line with tangled leaders, which ensnared the trout.

The ensuing argument developed to serious magnitude until Russell intervened by offering to examine the evidence as an uninterested third party. Russell inspected the lines and lures. When he announced his findings it seemed clear to whom the fish belonged. However, frustrated bickering continued between Tank and Chuck not only the rest of the day, but for the rest of their lives. To this day, Tank or Chuck can be provoked to defend their claim to this ensnared trout on cue by bar patrons for local entertainment. The element of suspicion is that Tank could describe his line (which was blue) but not his lure (he used either silver or gold lures), and Chuck not only described the silver lure but he also presented a duplicate silver lure from his pocket. The trout was hooked by a silver lure on a blue line. Therein lies the controversy.

In the middle of this fine expedition, in the middle of this fine day, in the middle of a particularly deep and rushing part of the Jefferson River, an astute one of the crew noticed a knothole the size of a slice of bologna in the side of the wooden dory that was bulging at its seam and leaking beads of water. If that plug were to give, there would be a gush of water that could cut a man in half. The hull would most likely split in two from the pressure. They all looked at the disk as if some radioactive grenade had fallen to the floor from outer space. The strained knothole was fret with sweat.

As was stated, Quimbley has a knack for assessing disaster. With authority, he directed the oarsman to steer for the nearest bank. Bubby somehow managed to swing the bow over. The dory slid to rest about 5 feet from the shore in shallow water. Like Viking arrivals, the men dispersed themselves and immediately sought bushes. Russell reviewed the situation while the others lightened the horde of solids (Vienna sausages, bananas, string cheese) and liquids (beer) by consuming them for the sake of safety. A reconsolidation of the necessary items (beer) made the dory much roomier than before. Now, only three people were permitted to ride in the boat at a time. The others had to wade along the bank, fishing downstream walking along to keep up with the dory. Once in a while, Russell would execute an exchange between floaters and waders, which allowed all of them to refresh their beer holding gullets.

All in all, a great time was had and many fish were caught that day. The Tub was deemed by everyone to be a fine fishing vessel, a boat to be reckoned with by professional standards. The only glitch in the day's events might have been Tank and Chuck's entanglement, though that situation proved entertaining as well.

At the end of the day, with light glowing in that golden glory characteristic of Montana dusk, the Tub landed at the BLM takeout and the men disembarked from her strained hull. She seemed relieved to be hoisted by human hands onto the waiting trailer. Water dripped from her belly marking the route from the banks of the Jefferson back up the highway to Quimbley's garage.

A few days later, Russell examined the knothole and scrapes against her hull. After assessment, he knew what he must do. He would seal the cracks, glue the trim, and disguise the leaking knothole with a thick coat of beautifying polyurethane: it was time to sell the Tub while she still floated.

So, if you see an advertisement seemingly too good to be true in the Thrifty Nickel for a hand-hewn wooden dory out of Ramsey, Montana, it's probably the Tub. However, despite the years of repair, veneer and cover up of structural damage, she's probably still seaworthy – a conclusion we've drawn in astonishment since we first doctored her knothole up, painted over the cracks and sold her to Russell Quimbley five years earlier.

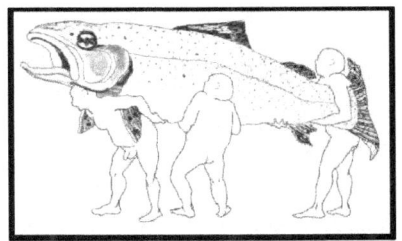

13. Fly Fishing a Super-Fund Site: Butte, Montana (by Michele White "Murray")

"The bountiful headwaters of the Clark Fork River"

Just outside of Butte, Montana traveling north on I-90, the highway passes through a landscape where the now defunct Anaconda Mining Company once processed thousands of tons of gold and silver ore sixty years ago. The disturbed landscape looks like Mars: bleak surfaces of sand and gravel are streaked with mineral stain and lie barren for long, eerie swaths where erosion and chemical burn have prevented plants from taking root. My huzbun and I intended to fish in this vicinity despite the historic mine tailings' federal classification as a super-fund site for reclamation. A friend of ours, who lives near the mining district, told us there are amazingly huge fish immediately below the tailings ponds. There, the combined bodies of the Silver Bow, Mill, Willow, and Warm Springs creeks form the headwaters of the Clark Fork River. Tony insisted we fish there with such conviction that we promised to investigate.

In preparation for wade-fishing this stretch, we read Fothergill & Sterling's, *"Montana Angling Guide,"* 1988. This book provides a harrowing account of the mining history and subsequent contamination of soil and water by sulfide mineral waste in the vicinity of Anaconda and Deer Lodge. They quoted some local fellow: *"There are enough chemicals in that river that you'll be able to catch a fish already cooked."* F&S made their point. We were afraid to enter the water for fear our waders might melt and our skin sizzle off our skeletons.

We drove north on I-90 and took the highway exit at Warm Springs, which is a small, sparsely populated town where the Montana State Mental Hospital is located. (Note-to-self: this facility is right across from a riparian habitat should we decide to retire there.) On the west side of the highway is the town of Warm Springs. On the east side, is a car tour with pamphlets and marked routes with parking beside scenic overlooks. ARCO (the mineral exploration company that used to own the mine many years ago), built an impressive car-touring route through the middle of the reclamation project.

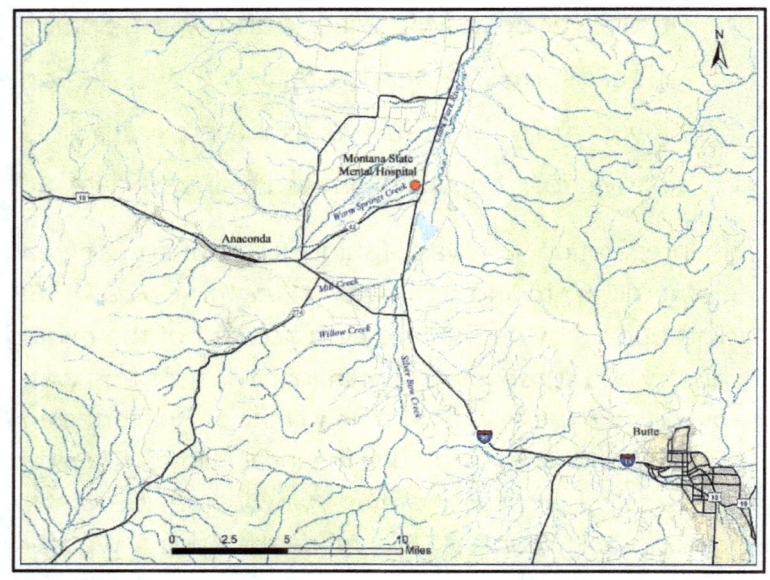

Anaconda reclamation site at the confluence of the Silver Bow, Mill, Willow, and Warm Springs creeks – headwaters of the Clark Fork River, Montana.

ARCO provided pamphlets in a dispenser at one of the roadside viewing stands. The literature explained the process of restoring the damaged plains to a healthy, riparian habitat. We followed the entire length of the loop and read how the toxic metals are (supposedly) being contained and their levels monitored by large holdings tanks in both wet and dry facilities, which we could see from the road.

This was useful information, in consideration that I've often wondered how mine tailings are dealt with in a reclamation project. The district had lain in a state of desolation for thirty years having been chemically burnt by acidic waters. The main source of contamination was derived from a waste pile of rock that had a lot of pyrite and other sulfides near where the old smelter used to stand. The smelter released toxic gases and rock with sulfides directly into the habitat through which, creeks meandered. The sulfides create acidic water when they get exposed to the atmosphere. This was in incredible lack of environmental foresight for the historic mining operations. In recent times, the EPA forced reclamation repercussions on ARCO as owners of the property, though they were not the operators of the smelter of many decades ago. As a result, ARCO was forced to address the tremendous task of reclamation in this area. Lucky them.

We arrived below the confluence of the three creeks and looked for steaming bones and rotting carcasses. There were no obvious signs of metallic poisoning. The meandering loops of the streams' waters were running shallow and sparkling clear below the enclosed tailings ponds. We decided to wear waders though the weather was oppressively hot, for fear of the chemical contents of the streambeds. We were afraid to let our dogs wade or drink the water, but there was little we could do about keeping them out of the stream.

At the time of this excursion, I had only been fly fishing twice since Doug first introduced me to the sport. As a consequence, I needed more time than he did to get my gear together. I fought with my gravel-guards and threading my guides while Doug selected a 7.5', #3-weight rod for me – one he had made himself. The rod was short, light, and fast for quick response inside the narrow confines of the overhanging canopy of willows. Casting was still difficult for me. The creek looked too shallow for our friend's conviction of large trout hiding there. The stream didn't look deep enough to host an animal larger than a pollywog.

Doug has been fly fishing for a long time and he can just about cast to a shrimp in a cocktail glass across the bar, (though that would be rude). In contrast, I needed to be as close to the fish as possible. My method was to lash my pathetic cast about wildly in the air until it fell reasonably close to my target. Any nearby shrubbery was an enemy: a snagging magnet for my line. I already dreaded the day's toil and did not expect to catch a fish, but dolefully entered the water. Doug disappeared, splashing softly downstream through the oxbows with our two dogs.

The previous day, I had already caught two nice trout on the Beaverhead River with our friend near Twin Bridges. So, this day, I didn't really care about casting perfectly or catching a fish. For this day, I intended to simply flop the fly about (a big Royal Wulff) and wade along appreciating the beauty of the river. At one bend with overhanging willows, I pulled back on the tippet with my fingers to load my rod like a fork with a wad of mashed potatoes and shot the line into the shadow under the overhanging branches. This ridiculous technique may have spooked a laughing trout out from under the foliage.

In this bored state, I waded along enjoying the scenery of underbrush, rabbits, deer, herons and beautiful ducks. I was surprised, by and by, to notice enormous, dangerously deep pools in the elbows of the stream's meanders. Big, dark shadows of some swimming things slipped around in there. I looked over the edge of one of these pools and saw slow torpedoes. Porpoises! Crazy large trout (I assume were trout) were hanging out in the deep pools. Mine-waste mutants! Eagerly, I plunked a fuzzy red and black Royal Wulff dry fly directly above one of the shadowy torsos. I didn't know, then, about the nature of fish and how they like their snacks to be presented from upstream in a natural, drag-free drift. The body of a huge finned-freak streaked across the shallow sandbar at my feet, leaving a wake on the surface where its back had gleaned. I felt slightly unnerved by its size and grateful it bolted away from me. I wondered if a fish might bite. Ridiculous, I know but I didn't know....

I continued wading downstream because the undergrowth along the bank was too dense to walk through. I waded softly and slowly, so as to avoid churning up the sediments with my boots. Eventually, Jessica (our old, silver-muzzled, black lab), joined me. She had been walking along the bank in the bushes and now wagged her tail at me from a place where the sandy bank was low enough for her to enter the stream. At her advanced age, she was reluctant to get her arthritic toes wet. I saw her ears flop forward as she focused on a grasshopper that had just landed onto the beach in front of her. With a startling flash, a huge trout slipped up on the bank and snagged the grasshopper in its jaws right in front of my dog! We were both shocked! Jessie stepped back, (she was once bit on the nose by a vole and has been timid of brave wildlife ever since.)

MY GOD! I must tell Doug about this! I didn't know a trout could snag something off the bank! First, though, GET OUT OF THE WATER AND AWAY FROM THE SCARY FISH! Movement through the dense bushery turned out to be hot, bothersome labor, especially in my hot waders. I staggered through the thickets, unintentionally flushing birds, deer and unidentified critters that made noisy scurries to get away from my twig-snapping campaign. I kept staggering and snagging my rod on the thickets. Soon, I was a sweating mess and was afraid of puncturing my waders. So, I returned to the water thinking I might have to bat at an aggressive trout with my rod if it came after me with an aggressive agenda. How did I know what a big trout might do when trapped?

I was wading downstream when a concussion exploded behind me. I screamed, though the loud thwack sounded vaguely familiar. I turned to look at the growing ring on the surface where some creature had breached. I also saw Fred, our other old dog, peering with lolling tongue, happy face, and wagging tail from a thicket of willows on the steep bank. He was smiling at the water where he had seen a furry aqueous mammal with a fleshy, flat tail come up to surprise me. I've heard of beavers dragging dogs underwater and drowning them, but I didn't know if a beaver would attack a small person or not. Now, I needed to get away from a big scary fish and an angry beaver, too, now. Wasn't this stream supposed to be polluted?

Beaver sneakin' up on me.

I finally spied Doug ahead of me, just in view. He was fishing in a wide bend where the river made a large, deep pool. I could see a school of fish sticking their snouts out of the riffle to look at him. I thought of "*Gold-eyes*" (*Hidodon alosoides*) because those type of fish bubble around on the surface and fool you into thinking they're trout, but they're not trout. Doug's buddies will demerit points if you catch a Gold-eye. Doug was cursing. That's why Fred and Jessie left him – they get nervous at the mention of certain words.

Doug was yanking at his snagged line from a mostly submerged log across the current from him. Fish were staring, embarrassed. I waited in case he wanted to be alone. He noticed me, though, then snapped his line off and muttered, "*Catch anything?*"

"*No,*" I answered. I didn't tell him I had not really been fishing with any true passion. I was a bit apathetic about trying to catch one.

"*Any hits?*" he asked.

"*No – But I saw a huge trout take a bug off the bank right in front of Jessica. He jumped out of the water to get a grasshopper. Jessie was scared! And there are beavers in here - big ones! Do you think a beaver would attack a human if it felt cornered? Are they territorial?*"

"*What kind of fly pattern are you using?*" He was ignoring my comments. Doug doesn't pay much attention to my stories. He rarely reads my articles, either. It's probably better that way. He is a man of few words and when he offers them, you better listen. He knows things.

Nowadays, I select my own flies and rig my own line. That day on the headwaters of the Clark Fork, Doug wanted me to catch a fish, despite my lack of ambition. He took my line and put a bead-head pheasant-tail dropper trailing about 15" behind a yellow grasshopper dry fly and instructed me to fish in this spot. He knew there were fish to be caught right here. He pointed where I should cast and told me how to cast. He explained the physical dynamics of the current and reminded me of the submerged stump. Then he left. I was not looking forward to casting with a backdrop of bushes behind me but I was assigned to catch a fish here.

I threw my pathetic cast upstream and played with the line giving the hopper gentle animate jerks to make it look like something I thought a trout should want to eat. This bend was a good place to stand because the inside shelf was shallow, broad and flat. Across from me, the main channel was deep and far enough away from my position that I shouldn't put any fish down with my presence. Mostly, though, I thought it unlikely that a beaver would climb up onto the shelf to attack me. At the least, I would be able to see a beaver coming.

Suddenly, I caught a fish. After that amazing surprise, I caught another. They were feisty Rainbow trout about ten inches long. Now I was having fun. The depth and steady stream of food made for consistent hits in this spot, just as Doug knew it would.

I practiced setting the hook. The trout spilt through the surface like bullets. (Once on the Bighorn, a Rainbow came spinning cartwheels so violently at us, we thought we needed to rig a trout-deflector on the bow of the dory.) I gently pulled the animals to me by stripping the line and then keeping them on the reel. I tried to release them underwater with as little bother as possible, (that is, if a trout doesn't consider it disturbing when his snack drags him across the channel by his lip to a lady wearing rubber pants.)

The trout were preferentially taking the pheasant-tail dropper over the hopper every time. Once in a while, I saw a large, spatula-sized dorsal fin swirl at the surface to bump my hopper. I was enjoying the action when I finally, (inevitably), snagged the submerged log. I lost the pheasant-tail dropper and was too lazy to tie another on. So, I decided to cast for the big fish that bumped my hopper.

I kept casting the grasshopper into the far current and mending the line, trying to keep that upstream flick from pulling my tippet under. I practiced roll-casting by using the downstream drag to load my rod tip. I flipped upstream and away from me to cast across the current into the far eddy. The hopper landed right up against the far bank into the shade where the water was deepest and the bank undercut. It lay on the surface without moving for a moment. Then, a fish took the fly for a fast deep swim. The line went suddenly taut and my tippet snapped. I assumed the trout must have pulled my line under the submerged log.

I rigged my line with another hopper and dropper combination and spent most of the afternoon in this one sweet spot. The sun was hanging low in the sky but the day was still hot. The shadows on the far bank grew in length over the surface of the eddy. I flung the hopper in the eddy again where the shadow lay. Then, I witnessed another extraordinary fish event: a mighty, huge Brown trout lifted its missile-like body out of the water to take a groggy, hot grasshopper off of a blade of grass overhanging the bank. This Brown was amazing – I wanted to catch that fish!

A whopping big trout picking a bug off the overhanging grass.

Probably every angler has a particular memory of the first really big fish they've ever caught. I'm biased now, but I think the first big fish ever caught by dry-fly, on your own without any help from anyone else, is an extraordinary sensation. My memory of that special event always takes me to below the tailings and treatment ponds of ARCO's reclamation project, to the headwaters of the Clark Fork and that wide bend. That wonderful hole full of fish is imprinted in my memory for later on when I'm an old lady unable to go to the river anymore (and, by then, probably living in Warm Springs at the Montana State Mental Hospital.)

I was casting with bad form and with no faith in myself. Miraculously, my line occasionally landed where it needed to be. Once in five casts or so, my fly drifted without drag as if someone else were in control. For one brief moment in the entire day, the grasshopper pattern twisted naturally on the surface. The riffle of the main current was sparkling with aged sunlight as the day disappeared on the horizon, and a great big beautiful Brown trout took my fly. I set the hook in amazement.

The big Brown ran downstream and deep. I played the line out through my fingers and kept my tip up. The reel went, "ZZZZZZzzzzz." He swam upstream and broke the surface just to look at me. I stripped the line fast as I could to try and get him back on the reel and nearly dropped my rod in the water. All my gear was flopping around and I had to trap my rod against my belly with my forearms but I kept the rod tip up. Beyond belief, I didn't lose the trout. Eventually, he tired of this rodeo and gave in to the force of my nagging line. I pulled his huge face alongside my leg. He was slightly over 18 inches long, (which is the length of my net) – a great hog of a fish. I was afraid to put my hand near his teeth, yet successfully clamped my hemostat on the hopper's shaft. The fish loosed himself from the crimped barb and swam back to his hole like a good, but maybe sullen, trout.

It was a magnificent day for fishing the headwaters of the Clark Fork! I was amazed at the contrast between devastation and reclamation in the vicinity of the Silver Bow, Mill-Willow and Warm Springs creeks. I don't know how efficiently the containment areas work, but for now, the confluence of the three streams that form the headwaters of the Clark Fork is functioning as a successfully reclaimed riparian habitat. It seems to be rehabilitated to the point of sustaining wildlife -and large trout for terrific fishing.

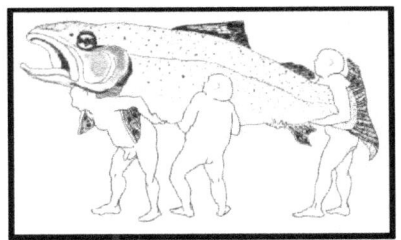

14. Salmon Flies on the Colorado (by Michele White "Murray")

"Big bugs in cow town tonight, boys."

Memorial Day weekend, we caught monster rainbow trout on the Colorado River during an adult stonefly event – not a hatch. It was a massive egg-laying carnival with clouds of huge salmon flies – giant stoneflies - so thick in the air they blackened the sun like locusts. Dogs shivered. Trout strained their necks to stare at the big bugs in the sky. People with limp worms on limp lines asked us as we hauled the trout aboard, "Hey, what're you using?" We pulled the prehistoric insects off our faces for display and answered, "These!"

I never saw anything like it before. Salmon flies are large, creepy stoneflies (*Califiornica Pteronarcys*) with stickery little feet on the ends of long, jointed legs. Rafting guides examined the mysterious bugs that were landing on their tourists' hats. My sister, who hadn't brought her glasses to the river, was poking her nicely painted fingernail into a stonefly's rump that had landed on her paddle handle. She observed in her blurred vision the characteristic, throbbing, orange stripe on a stonefly's back. She provoked the critter to make it flash its colorful signal for all to see.

Salmon Fly close-up.

Doug told me that the adult salmon flies don't come out very often, that most of the time only the nymphs are active. Apparently, there is no pupa-emerger stage with the stonefly like we're familiar with caddis and mayflies. Some species of stonefly/salmon fly nymphs live up to 3 years in the water before they mature. Eventually, the nymph climbs out of the river and clings to a rock. When they're good and dry they bust out of their crackly shells and emerge as fully formed adults. Thus, witnessing adult stonefly/salmon fly activity is rare and certainly not something to rely upon for angling. But, when the adults are active, the really big trout come up from their murky depths and feed exclusively on them – kind of like responding to having free doughnuts at the office. Doug knew that when adult salmon flies are seen on the river, it's time to catch really large fish.

Shortly after we arrived in our vehicle at the confluence of the Colorado River with Sheephorn Creek near Radium, a large, fairly grimy man came over to us with a plastic ice cooler in his paw. He opened the lid and held it out to us without further explanation. In the cooler was a strange sight. The bottom was lined with half-eaten food in dirty Baggies, a package of cigarettes, and a long twig with leaves. Against the sides were some dying salmon flies the size of hummingbirds. The most significant item to view was an enormous, 20-inch Rainbow trout fat as my leg, lying in a curl of rigor mortis. It was a sad sight.

We thanked the guy, though, for sharing his glory with us and congratulated him for his trophy catch. He left pleased with himself (for either showing off his fish or for totally disgusting us – I'm not sure which effect he was seeking.) Doug asked me,

"*Did you see what he had in there?*" and I answered,

"*Yeah, a fish horror chamber*", and Doug said,

"*Salmon fly adults – really big fish come up for those!*"

I looked at my husband, whose voice I did not recognize: Doug was unusually excited in his usually quite way. His eyes glowed.

We were putting our raft in the river at Radium with a group of friends and family in their brand new raft. Despite the excitement of these bugs in the air, we were suffering a bit of trepidation about floating from Radium to Rancho because at that time of year, spring run-off is a significant factor in running Yarmony (Hoyt's) Rapids. We expected the water to be too big for our dory, so we brought our self-bailing raft instead. Our intentions were to go first and buddy-spot for our friends through their first run of Yarmony whitewater.

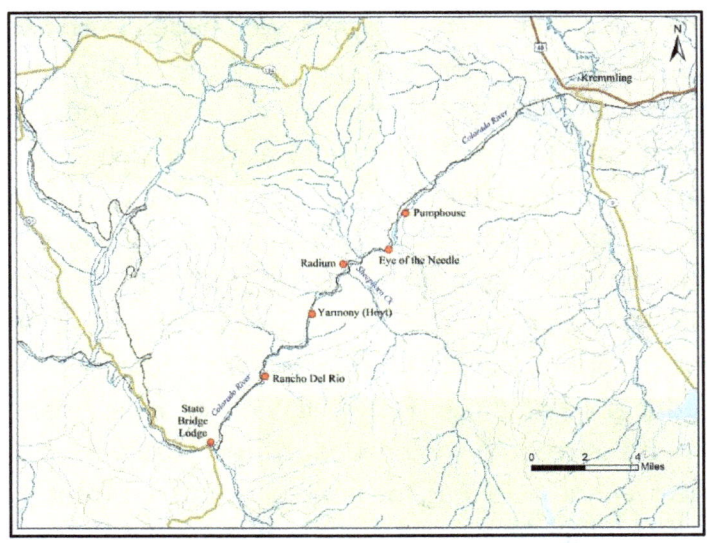

Upper Colorado River rapids and access areas.

Doug riggin' up our new boat.

This being their maiden voyage, we needed to christen the vessel. The men found a river virgin (novice to rafting) for good luck to bless the bow of their new raft with a can of Hamm's beer. She wasn't the prettiest river virgin, (being a bit older than color television and seeming a little dour about getting wet), but she was the prettiest one they found standing on the bank in the rain. The river was actually really low, running at 500 cubic feet per second. River virgin was not enthusiastic about going rafting in the rain and even less happy when she realized she needed to wade halfway across the river and help drag the boat to the main current. We wrapped her up in rain gear and tightened her life-vest extra snug to show our appreciation. Then, the regatta headed downstream: Doug and I with our oar-frame and the others with yellow paddles pulling in the current against the rain and wind.

Doug and I didn't take our rods out of their cases at first. Sour, unspoken tension rested on our tongues in anticipation of the upcoming rapids. Doug noodled apprehension between his fingers. We watched our buddies practice the maneuvers they would need to execute in the upcoming rapids. Their collaborated efforts resulted in slow spins and stagnant attempts to cross the current. I overheard crabby snippets of criticism flung at their skipper. They seemed seriously mutinous. Then, we heard the growing roar of Yarmony rapids coming from around the bend and Doug asked me with a nervous voice,

"Just stay left, right?"

"Right, left." I answered.

Before we descended onto the dropping tongue of water that rolls into Yarmony, everyone tightened their brand-new lifejackets and lashed down bags and coolers. The others double and triple checked their emergency gear, (things like extra paddles and throw-lines were ready in case someone got sucked overboard by a thunderous wave). Doug and I shot ahead and anchored onto a rock along the shore so we could scout the rapids ahead on foot. We climbed high to overlook the slot at Yarmony. There was nothing there! The water was so low that we could have walked across. As the new raft entered Yarmony, Doug popped a can of Ol' Milwaukee's finest and drank it rather than watch the new raft team enter the canyon. Our buddies paddled like madmen and bumped off of every rock in the channel. They turned their heads around to watch us watching them. Then, they just stopped paddling and allowed their craft to migrate slowly through Yarmony, eventually exiting backwards from the chute.

Not worried at Hoyt's after all.

All fear having dissipated, we followed after them easily. The only tricky maneuver was for Doug to find enough room in the water to dig his oars in between the rocks. A couple lateral moves were required to avoid going over big submerged boulders and small hydraulic holes. Doug executed the moves with slow deliberation. No rocks kissed our baffles.

After Yarmony, the fishing was ON! I looked up at the sky to welcome the newly emerging Sun and to thank the River God for not swallowing my family. That's when I saw THEM as a cloud for the first time - adult salmon flies in aerial ballet! They were high in the sky, not like caddis or mayflies. Salmon fy adults fly way up where eagles and hawks go, like biplanes in combat. It was a cyclone of quad-winged bugs!

Cyclone of salmon flies overhead.

I unzipped the sleeve of my rod casing and found that Doug had already rigged our rods with adult salmon fly patterns. First cast - *BOOM!* A big rainbow bent my 8.5-foot, #5-weight rod in half. I lost my hemostats trying to handle the big hog-of-a-trout. Another cast - *BOOM!* I lost Doug's hemostats in the trout rodeo, too! After catching a load of rainbows, most of which were quite large, Doug and I traded positions so he could fish - and we were only halfway into the morning!

Our rafting companions paddled slowly ahead and cheered at us each time we caught a fish until they got tired of cheering and finally just ignored our action all together. Eventually, they abandoned us. We used the same dry fly all day long until it was so battered it didn't even look like a stonefly anymore. The hackle was gone and the hook had been pulled straight and re-bent so many times that the metal had become malleable. I clipped the unraveling thread and reforming the hook and the fish kept taking it. The largest fish came out of a wide, boiling, turbulent bend in the middle of the river. I didn't see where my fly hit the surface, but a magnificent fish took it for a long, deep run.

At the end of two days fishing between Pumphouse and Rancho Del Rio (Eye of the Needle rapid was also non-negotiable due to extremely low water), we probably caught 50 enormous rainbow trout between us. Even the whitewater rafting enthusiasts started fishing. We exclusively used large adult stonefly patterns with orange markings or large orange stimulators (size 6 - 10) to catch fish. On the second day, the leader slipped off my line due to the failure of one of those plastic sleeve connectors. So, I grabbed a reel off Doug's streamer rod. I fished with the heavier, #6-weight line on my lighter rod and just slapped at the water. The thick streamer leader was only about one meter long and in shabby condition, all knotted and kinked, but the fish were still taking my dry fly – not very picky, these trout!

When we finally left the Colorado, we knew we had experienced a very special event and I wondered if this would be one of those once-in-a-lifetime experiences. When we returned the following weekend the adult stonefly rendezvous was over. The enormous trout sank with their stuffed bellies back to the depths where they usually hang-out, probably lounging around in their fleece underwear burping smelly stonefly belches. Only normal-size Brown trout were to be had.

I don't have any idea how regularly the salmon fly adults come off the Colorado River, but I know it's not very often. So, if you see great clouds of quad-winged furry bugs with orange stripes on their backs, you would really be missing some exciting sport if you did not rig yourself a fly rod with a salmon fly pattern. I guarantee – it'll be FISH ON all day long!

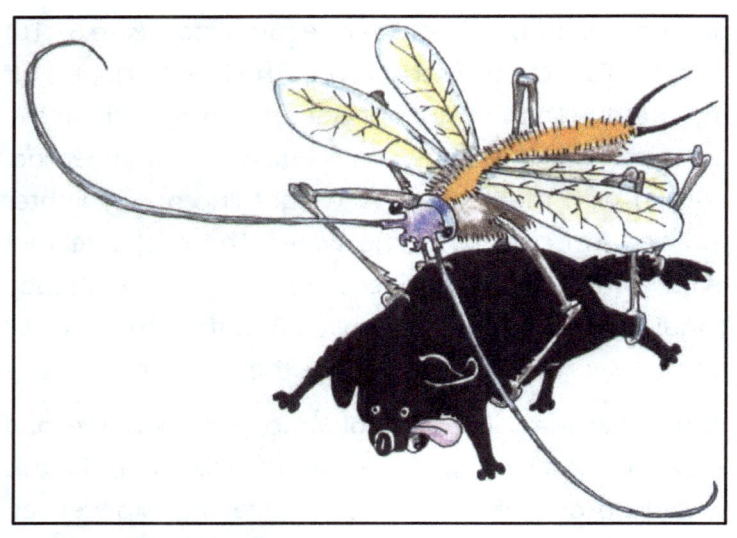

Salmon flies big enough to carry off yer dog.

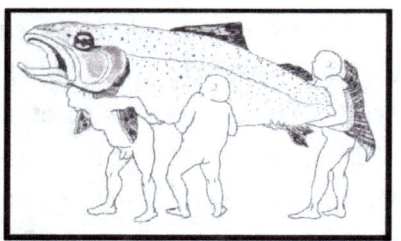

15. Cochetopa Creek

It's all about mortality: everything's about mortality – mortality is about mortality."

Have you ever covertly examined your spouse when they're not looking and wondered who they REALLY are? 'Hmm, look at that white hair. Do we both have white hair growing out of our ears? What about that extra skin hanging under the chin now and new lines around our eyes? How long has that been going on? What will life will be like without him? Who will go first, I wonder?' I have done this – stared at my huzbun and wondered these things – especially recently. We were on a road trip driving to a personal place special to Doug near Gunnison. He was scheduled for surgery on Monday and the apprehension was so unsettling to us both that we could not concentrate on much else going on. Apparently, we are entering an age when mortality starts coalescing from an imaginary boogey man into a realistic presence in our lives.

When the love of my life dog, Banjo, was diagnosed with cancer in 1998, I was inconsolable. I wasn't ready for this loss and I didn't have a plan for a world without this fur-person beside me. Doug understood this irrational, immeasurable love for a dog but he didn't know what to do for me so he took us on meandering road trips in central Colorado on the backroads to console my grieving heart. He shared his most secret places with me – places that made him feel better, places that are good for the soul. He found these places as a younger man when he was a student at Western State in Gunnison. He explored the great expanse of open wilderness in Gunnison and Lake Counties in order to look for something - something inspiring to himself and intimate to a single young man in his twenties. In my pain, I only remembered these landscapes and camping spots as a vague blur. The photos we took during that time are of a sad woman sitting next to streams staring at her dying dog surrounded by the magnificent beauty of Nature's Grace.

Now, we headed for these places again before his surgery day. I remembered the basic region in the rolling hills driving on deserted dirt roads, but Doug knew the exact turn-offs on wheeled tracks that led through wide-open range without fences or telephone poles: wild places. Thigh-high sage and juniper bushes studded the faces of alluvial fans that draped higher topographic ridges dotted with cedar and fir trees. In these open spaces only the ponderosa and families of aspen knew we were here, as if they were waiting to see who would arrive. The trees were used to the footsteps of the elk who move through their branches, or bear, or rabbits and grouse. In the basin of this valley a dendrite of the Cochetopa creek (always of one, sole River, connected to all other rivers, ongoing, flowing past Time) cold snow-melted water meandered through small elbows between red willow-lined banks. Red volcanic rock uplifted to the sky in massive cliffs for the hawk, eagle and cougar to perch. We found our place near a waterfall where dogs can run amuck and where the brook trout wallop the surface of the riffles for midges, mayflies and grasshoppers. This is what you do. This is where you go when you are troubled. Doug taught me that.

The Ute of Colorado knew this place before Doug and I arrived, though they were not the first people in this basin to fish on this creek. Before the Ute there were unnamed Neolithic people who followed two predominant animals through these hills during the Holocene. The animals were the Miocene-aged elk (C. canadensis nelson) and an even longer lineage of "buffalo" – technically "bison" – (from an evolution of Bison latifrons to Bison antiquus to Bison occidentalis to Bison bison...). The elk and buffalo had been in this region long before humanoids arrived with dogs pulling travois (or Ford pickups toting slide-in campers). The elk and bison were here in this basin grazing while people were still struggling to walk upright and hold tools and make baskets to carry water on another continent. The Ute, however, provided the vocal iteration (only 1,500 years ago) that now stands for the name of this region: Cochetopa, meaning, "Pass of the Buffalo".

I don't know if it's my native ancestry or if I am a little "touched', but my blood boils when I am in such a pristine human-appealing habitat. I am always aware of the Ancient Ones who came before us, those who stood here, those who walked and hunted for berries, those who sat on this rock and made the human stuff that they can use for their daily survival. I walk in their footsteps and sit on the same boulder and look around me at the Cochetopa creek drainage. You can come across evidence of their having been here at all: an arrow head underfoot, a trail winding on the most convenient path between the boulders from the rim of the valley to the creek below, a flat stone that fits in your hand just so. These are evidence of those who came before me, of those who also stopped on their journey in this place and nourished their souls, taking time to let their bodies heal and their babies grow. All of us animals who came here to this place take some time in our life to rest for a while. Time waits.

Sometimes people get into squabbles with the person they love. That's as natural with time as growing trophy ear hairs. I've learned that when the right person aligns with you it really is for life, like a celestial event in the solar system. There is no escaping when you meet your right mate. That is why no matter how long I work away from home, no matter how far away, or how trying times can be, I know that Time will find us both wearing thermal underwear inside of our waders, hiking in the chilly morning dew up to our crotches in sage under wide open skies strung out along the bank of a creek barely within each other's view. One will be casting dry flies to a riffle, the other will be nymphing through a dark pool. We might be in Idaho, maybe Montana or even near our home in central Colorado but we will be together because this is as it should be. This is the life we have created. Like those who came before us, we are grateful to have a place to restore our seat in this universe.

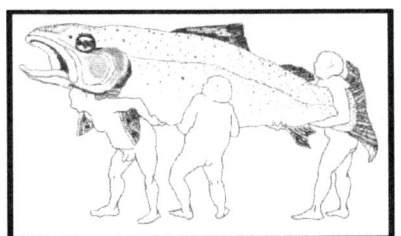

16. Autumn on the Dolores: An October Odyssey (by Al Marlowe)

It may be with some reluctance that you think about spending a long day drive from almost anywhere in Colorado to get to a fishing venue as special as the Dolores River, but you will be even more reluctant to leave.

Summer in Colorado means fishing. The runoff is over, streams are low and clear, and the fish hungry for a well presented dry-fly. Summer is that all-too-short a period of time that anglers dream about all winter. It is also vacation time. The highways are filled with cars from every state in the nation and many of the cars are filled with fishermen. Anglers from here and there stand shoulder-to-shoulder in streams and along lakeshores, tangling their back-casts with those of other nearby anglers. Summer is chaotic.

Wouldn't it be great to fish the famous rivers of the west and have them all to yourself; to pull into a streamside campground and find it empty? Or, to fish a stream full of two and three-pound cutthroats, eager to take your fly? No, this is not the impossible dream. This scenario can be enjoyed, even in Colorado. Just wait until October. The Dolores River may be just the place to take delight in your odyssey.

Having heard stories of this new fishery, Larry Stankiewicz, of Littleton, Colorado, with whom I've shared many days fishing, was eager to check out the river.

"*My neighbor said to use any dry-fly size 12 or 14,*" he told me. Anxious to see if such tales were true, we departed early last October on our odyssey.

The Dolores heads in the San Juan Mountains on the south slope of Mount Wilson. It runs southwest parallel to State Highway 145 until reaching the town of Dolores. Here, the river turns to flow northwest, entering a deep canyon cut into sandstones of the Mesa Verde. For the next hundred or so miles, the Dolores is a canyon stream, its channel carved in red, peach tan and purple colored sedimentary rocks, dating back to the Triassic Age.

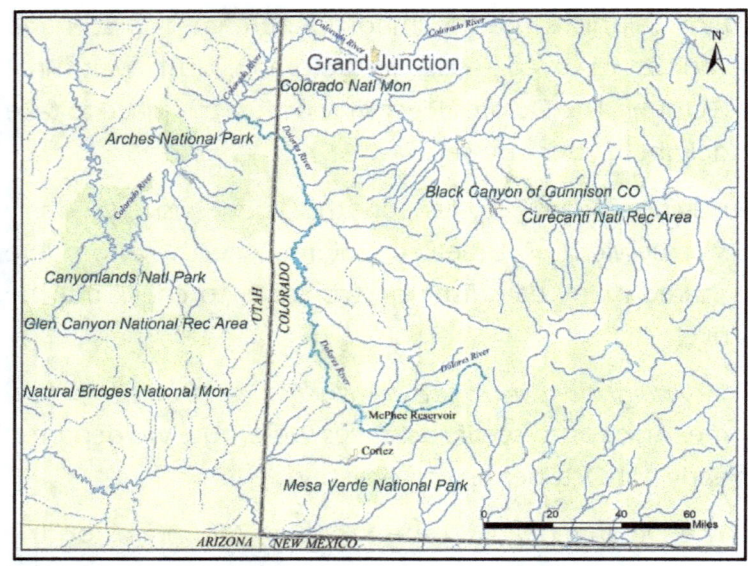

Location of the Dolores River in southwest Colorado.

In 1985, 270-foot high McPhee Dam was completed. On rare occasions, a dam is beneficial to a stream. McPhee went further. It created a fishery. Below the dam, a mild year around climate and relatively stable water temperatures have combined to create a trout haven.

Fishing in the Dolores prior to building McPhee was fair at best. Occasionally, a fish up to five pounds would be taken. Most were much smaller. Now the Dolores River has become one of Colorado's newest hot-spots for trout fishing. Opened to anglers in 1990, this river yields rainbows and Snake River cutthroats in the 20-inch class. Stream improvement work was implemented by the

Colorado Division of Wildlife and Trout Unlimited, enhancing habitat. It is now home to feisty browns as well as cutthroats and rainbows. Restricted fishing methods and catch-and-release regulations protect the resource for future anglers.

In October, there is no need to rise early; no need to be out on the water at dawn. Nights are cool, in the 40s, making good sleep-in weather. It takes a while to warm up the canyon and the bugs and the fish. The sun doesn't touch the river for a couple of hours past dawn.

Morning is time for a leisurely breakfast and removing the last bit of sleep from your eyes with a second cup of coffee. It's a time to walk the trail along the stream and observe. Look into the clear stream and ponder how so many large fish can hide in water that seems to have few hiding places. Watch a merganser paddle downstream, beak in the water, searching for his breakfast. Notice the deer tracks in the soft river sand, evidence that camp had visitors during the night.

As the sun begins to warm the water, arousing the fish's appetites, they seem to materialize here and there. In front of a rock, that a few minutes before, was empty water, a brown was now waiting impatiently, like a hungry diner in a fast food joint. Riffles that were barren earlier now held more fish than a hatchery pond.

Wildlife is abundant along the Dolores. Visitors tell of hearing wild turkeys noisily scratching in the scrub oak.

Mule deer cross the river in full view of an angler. We were lulled to sleep with the mournful wailing of coyotes and awakened by the raucous song of the pinion jay. As we waded along the banks of the stream, the sounds of wild critters could be heard in the streamside scrub oak, noisily scratching unseen in the dry fallen leaves. Wild turkeys, perhaps?

With 10 or 11 miles of river to fish, how should an angler go about selecting a fishin' hole? We found it to be a simple task. First, we found a place to set up camp. Then, we fished the river beside camp. Three days of exploring several miles of stream indicated that one run was as good as another. This is not to suggest that anglers who fish here often won't have favorite holes. We found, though, that below the dam, there are a lot of fish and one run had as much to offer as another.

Wanting to see what the river had to offer other than around our camp, Larry and I drove upstream toward the dam. In a tail water-pool, about a hundred yards long, we could see the sulking forms of fish holding in the slow current. Periodically, one would leave its position to take some small, unseen insect from the surface and return to wait for more.

Even though the fall hatches did not include any large insects to suggest using large flies, Humpys turned out to be a good pattern. A No. 12, tied with natural deer hair produced fish of up to 19 inches. When fish can be seen rising aggressively all around and the water's surface has an absence of bugs, emergers fished just under the surface are often a logical choice. Tiny RS-2's in size 18 or 20 did produce fish at such times, although the fall weather made things go a bit slowly. The gin-clear water probably was not much help, either. Nymph fishermen may want to try a Gold Ribbed Hare's Ear or scup patterns in tan or green. As with many streams, the key to success is having a variety of patterns in a variety of colors.

In one run I fished, the water by the far bank was shallow and fast. The rippled surface effectively hid a fish only a few feet away. After drifting a No. 12 Humpy next to the bank a few times, it disappeared. No rise form. No splash. Just a steady, determined pull on the 5x leader let me know where the fly went. 10 minutes later, a three-pound Snake River cutthroat was my reward. I gently removed the Humpy and watched the fish swim back to his hole, perhaps a bit wiser.

The 11-mile section of the river below McPhee Dam has been designated as catch-and-release water. Fishing is permitted with flies and lures only and all fish caught must be returned to the water, unharmed immediately. If photos are needed, have your partner get some of you playing the fish. Avoid keeping it out of the water any longer than necessary to unhook it.

While the Dolores is open most of the year, water released from the reservoir in May and June sometimes makes the river unfishable then. By July, the river is more hospitable. Between December 1 and March 31, the road is closed to vehicles to protect the deer and elk on their winter range and birthing grounds. During this time, some fishermen use cross-country skis to fish open water below the dam.

Flies produce well on the Dolores. Long rods and fine leaders (4x - 7x) are dictated by conditions that are usually low and clear in October. The river is fairly wide and open enough that back-casts won't be snagging on low branches and streamside brush.

The river is wadeable and can be crossed in many places with hip boots but chest waders will allow the angler to work the deeper holes easier. The current is slow but the bottom tends to be a bit slick because of moss on the rocks.

There are two developed camping facilities along the Dolores River below McPhee Reservoir. The first is Bradfield campground about 30 miles northwest of the town of Dolores. From Dolores, travel west on Highway 145 for 2 miles. Go right on Highway 184 for 8 miles. Turn right on U.S. Hwy 491 for 13 miles, then go right on Forest Road 505 for 1 mile. The campground is large and open with an easy to access boat ramp and trailer parking. This area can be quite busy during the short rafting season on the Dolores River (usually just several weeks around Memorial Day weekend).[1]

The second developed camping facility is at Ferris campground. There are latrine-type of compost toilets and water spigots but no trash pickup. During winter season, the toilets are open but the water is turned off. The Ferris campground is located a couple of miles downstream of the McPhee Dam. In October, you can have the place to yourself.

Camping at Ferris Campground along the Dolores River in mid-October.

There are also a few non-developed campsites along the road's shoulder. The more pleasant ones are at the river's bank. Some sites are secluded in cottonwood groves and bramble thickets. Remains of an old homestead decorate

---

[1] For detailed info about conservation of this river, refer to https://doloresriverboating.org/

one site. Old farm buildings and hay stacks are scattered in the meadows along the road.

The Dolores is a long drive from almost anywhere in Colorado. From Denver, the trip is an all-day event; 10 hours' worth. To make the long trip worthwhile, allow several days.

From Durango, go west on US 160 past the entrance to Mesa Verde National Monument, to Cortez, then north 26 miles on US 666 to Cahone. If you're coming from Grand Junction, go south on US 50 to Whitewater, about five miles from Junction. Turn off onto Colorado 141 and continue to US 666, about a four-hour drive. Continue on to the intersection of 141 and US 666. Go south, past Dove Creek, to Cahone.

Once at Cahone, turn east on a blacktop road on the north side of town. A sign at the turn says, "*San Juan National Forest Access.*" In about three miles, it dead-ends at Road 16, marked by a BLM sign pointing south stating - "*Dolores River Access 2.6 Miles.*" It doesn't say that you must turn east again in a mile. You must. From here, Forest Service Road 504 winds downhill to the Bradfield Bridge, where it crosses the Dolores. Follow FS 504 up the hill across the river to FS 505 and turn right. Follow it south along the east side of the river. On the east side of the river, signs provide fishing, access and camping information.

For flow information, contact the Dolores River Boating Advocates (doloresriverboating.org). The minimum flow below McPhee Dam is to be 78 cubic feet per second and a flow of 150 may be optimal for fishing.

Recommended minimum flows for floating are:

- 200 cfs for canoes / kayaks / inflatables
- 800 cfs for small rafts to 14 feet
- 1000 cfs for large rafts to 18 feet

The flow rates are controlled by Bureau of Recreation releases from McPhee Reservoir.

Fly shops in Durango and Dolores can provide more information on fishing the Dolores, including hatches and patterns to use. Guide service is also available through shops and from local guides. Restaurant meals, lodging, groceries, gas and fishing licenses can be purchased in Durango, Dolores and Cortez.

Larry and I spent three enjoyable days on the Dolores. While the fishing had been slow, the pleasant weather and solitude made up for the sparse action. We spoke to only two or three other anglers in that time. It was with some reluctance that we packed the trailer and prepared for the long drive home.

As we pulled out of our camp site, the river seemed to say, *'Stay a while longer.'* Unfortunately, jobs in Denver were insisting that we return. We drove slowly along the river, wondering if perhaps we should have tried this bend or that long, slow pool.

'*Maybe we should stay an extra day,*' I thought, as we headed up the hill from the Bradfield Bridge.

The Dolores River is a place where an autumn angler can enjoy an odyssey. Even though it is located on an excellent Forest Service road, it receives few visitors in this season. In October, the weather is pleasant. Biting insects are gone. Daytime temperatures in the 70's mean shirtsleeve comfort. Cool nights mean bright colors on streamside brush. And October means fishing in solitude.

The Dolores River looking upstream from Bradfield Campground in mid-October.

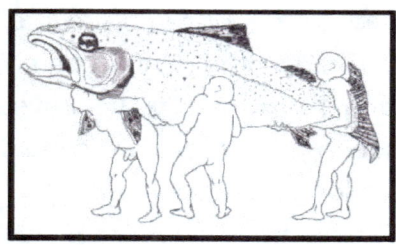

17. The San Juan River below Navajo Dam, New Mexico (by Michele White "Murray")

"Sometimes diversions from fishing make the fishing trip extra special, even if it is a super fishing venue."

We like to fish the San Juan River at Navajo Dam in New Mexico not only for the large trout, but also for the canyon landscape and one particular unique element of being in this part of New Mexico: Simon Canyon day hike with the dogs. This morning hike makes the San Juan River much more attractive to visit than just for enjoying the world class fishing.

A significant factor in fishing the San Juan River below the Navajo dam in New Mexico is that this tail water is the Mecca of Western American Gentlemen's (formal old guys) Fly Fishing venues. There is no need to feel intimidated by this aspect, (there are hard core women anglers there as well as young people and first-timers). It is simple to appreciate an old world etiquette in order for everyone to enjoy this unique, amazing habitat chock full of HUGE-OLA gigantic trout. If you want to participate in the angling of these porpoise-sized trout at Texas Hole or immediately below the dam in famous holes with names like "Lunker Alley", you will be standing shoulder-to-shoulder with some to the worlds' most seasoned trout veterans - all of this pressure because the trout are selectively (and voraciously) feeding on teeny eeny weeny little black midge larvae and scuttling around between your feet looking for scuds like pigs looking for truffles. This is no story teller's exaggeration.

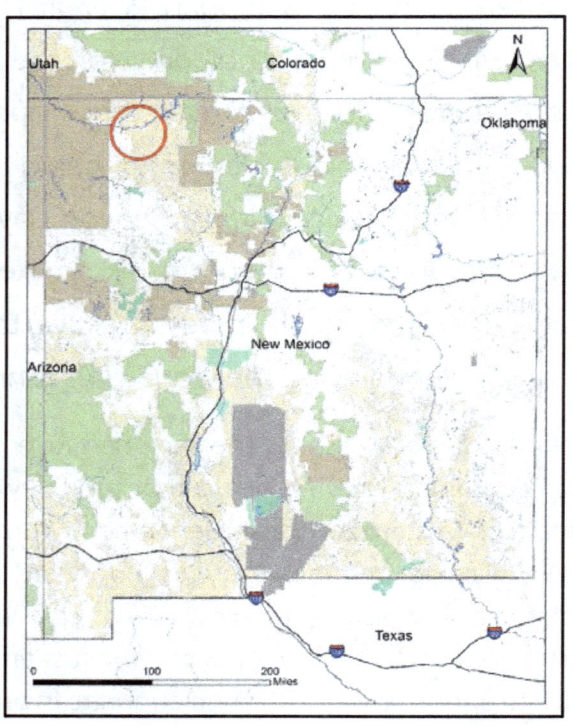

Location of the San Juan River Tailwaters below Navajo Dam, New Mexico.

The San Juan River tailwaters area below Navajo dam is considered to be a remote fly fishing destination venue by some angler's standards, as it is fairly far off from a major interstate. That said, the location is easy to find without much detail in following directions if you are willing to drive through dry, arid, cedar and sage kind of mundane terrain for a few hours. The ideal time to go is probably fall or winter because the summer in northern New Mexico can be oppressively hot (for people as well as for our dogs).

Even in autumn, the Canyonlands will still be warm (upper 70's and 80's) in the day and cool (frost) at night. December through February can be treacherously cold with icy winds blowing up river and yet still yield a lovely warm, sunny day in the upper 60's. The water from Navajo Reservoir is uncomfortably cold, so wearing thick neoprene waders would be an asset for wade fishing. I wear thermal underwear inside my regular gauge waders and layers of upper clothing so I might shed layers if the day becomes too hot and then replace the layers as the day becomes cold again.

The popular attraction of fishing the San Juan River tailwaters below Navajo Reservoir is the size and abundance of trout, with pods of them visibly feeding seemingly without any apprehension about the humans standing near them. The phenomenon of huge trout at tail water locations is based on the stability in flow and temperature. Insects – in particular midges and mayflies

- thrive under these conditions and provide a steady stream of food year around for the trout with less stress for scavenging. The result is a localized population of finned hogs.

The San Juan River is known for an odd hydraulic feature called Texas Hole. This is a large eddy that slowly flows upstream on the parking lot side of the river and then flows downstream as slowly on the far side. The result is that boats can launch from the parking lot, float upstream, cross the river to float downstream, then cross the river and float upstream again and do this all day long. Where else can boats put in and take out at the same place? It's funny to see all the many colored boats floating like a slow carousel around in this large eddy. The site would seem ridiculous if people weren't so easily catching and landing huge trout with their nymphing rigs.

Maybe the oddity of floating around the same circle with a bunch of other people all day seems too silly to us, but both my huzbun and I like to do a couple of turns on the carousel at Texas Hole then move on floating downstream. We leave the flotilla behind and are usually only one of a couple boats committed to floating the rest of the day to cover the two or three miles further downstream to other river access points. It doesn't take all day to float 2 miles, it's just that there are so many large trout along the way and catching them all is a time consuming occupation.

When we first arrive at Navajo Dam on our drive, we can see the river and all of the famous fishing holes below us. That is because we arrive from the north side of the reservoir and our access is to drive down the face of the dam to the river. The first site of the river is always mesmerizing. Even in winter people are standing in the river like bears in Alaska lined up to snag a salmon.

Tiny fishermen as seen from above the Navajo Dam.

Of course, being Colorado residents, we have to control our excitement and drive by the river access until we buy our out of state licenses. Though there are multiple fly shops waiting for your patronage, we have been going to Abe's fly shop at the gas station in the town of Navajo

Dam for 20 years. It is not likely we will take our business across the street simply because the people at Abe's have always provided great advice, reasonable prices, and a variety of goods that we need to replenish our camper for the week. We are loyal customers for those reasons. To us, going into Abe's for advice on which fly pattern to use and to buy out of state licenses is part of the routine, part of the tradition, and part of the magic spell that befalls us on this river.

Also, we fish with dogs. (Why would anyone bring dogs to the San Juan River? That is another entire article). Ideally, we like to camp in undeveloped campsites so the dogs can enjoy some freedom off the leash. That is not possible at the San Juan River. Though lovely, camping along the San Juan below the dam is limited to the Cottonwood Campground. Despite the limitation of staying in a numbered lot, the positive side includes amiable camp hosts, clean, dry, warm bathrooms with running water and flushing toilets, trash service, spigots of running water around the campground, clean fire pits, picnic tables, and river access. The campground is beautiful with huge thick cottonwood trees providing shade and scenery. Sometimes, when we go in winter, we are the only ones staying there. Otherwise, it would be a good idea to make reservations in advance so as to ensure a spot to stay on the river. If you can't stay in the Cottonwood Campground, then you have to stay in one of the rather dour motels or asphalt campgrounds back in town.

Cottonwood Campground.

For flies, both Doug and I will opt to use dry flies rather than nymph for just about any venue even if, such as in this case, nymphing is the proven best method for catching more fish and larger fish. The San Juan is, of course, very well documented for success with nymphing rather than using dry flies. That said we both still go to Abe's fly shop to buy our out-of-state licenses and ask them what kind of flies are working. The answer is mostly the same: really tiny tiny itty bitty black midge larvae and / or black midge mergers. The sizes are so small (size 22 – 26), that I have to use my "readers" to count them in the little plastic cup as I buy them. Tying them on the line is a whole other challenge as well. Using these microscopic flies is another reason one might want to hire a guide – or – bring someone under the age of 40 along.

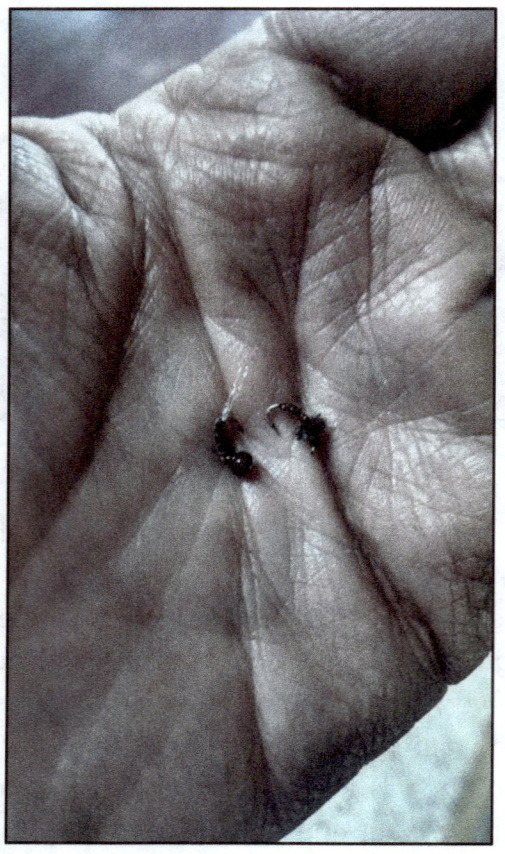

Teeny tiny dark fly patterns.

After we buy our teeny eeny weeny patterns, #7 and #8 tippet, and a new hat or T-shirt, we go claim a campsite at Cottonwood Campground, then address our fishing set-ups. This means new leaders with #7 to #8 filament tippet and one of the subatomic particle sized midge emerger patterns (black with a foam head). Then, we attach an even tinier quark-sized midge larva pattern that looks like a punctuation mark from a 1950's typewriter. The idea is you can walk along the river from the campground all the way up to Texas Hole (about 2.5 miles). Along the way, watch for rising fish (giant huge manatee-sized rainbows) sipping at the surface. When you find them, you can simply enter the water and start casting gently to them. They will not leave.

The feeding trout will continue to sip at the surface and wobble to the left or right to snack on the naturals flowing with the current under the water. They don't care if people are there, as long as you aren't stepping on their heads. As a matter of fact, if you stay in one spot trout will eventually move to your downstream ankle to begin feeding on the silt your feet are churning up. You can attract a whole army of trout at your side this way. Totally crazy!

The technique in catching one of the monsters (and by monsters I mean that the trout are thick, heavy and large – easily 18+ inches and in abundance with 20-inch + specimens as well) – to catch them, you view the foam line or current they are feeding on and get a sense or count the time it takes for them to rise. Then, you cast without a snap or plop – land gently like fairy dust on their line. Time your cast so that there is no need to mend prior to the fly going over their snout. Let the fly and line lie without any drag until it passes over their head and then beyond them even if the line sinks before you retrieve it. I have had trout take the emerger on the swing when the line and fly is underwater.

Things that will make a trout suspicious:
1. Wrong fly
2. Wrong size
3. Visible line
4. Visible tag ends of tippet at the knot
5. Raggedy fly (unraveling)
6. Drag

Otherwise, if you have the right fly, the right size, thin tippet, and a clean drift – you are going to catch a large trout and a lot of them, like following a cookie recipe. If you are willing to opt for less fish or smaller fish, a simple common pattern that is easier to tie on, easier to cast, and easier to see (mayfly, caddis, stonefly, Royal Wulff, BWO) will work to catch more "normal-size" trout, especially if you glide your fly across the top of a riffle or land it against the bank.

Parked to fish a riffle on the San Juan.

There is a very odd almost unforgivable situation I am reluctant to share but I must in order to introduce my favorite reason for going to the San Juan River: the embarrassing topic is a sense of "almost-boredom" with catching large fish over and over again all day long. The reason I feel so badly is for fish. At a super popular venue like the San Juan River, the trout are likely caught over and over again. You can tell by the way they respond when you catch them – they'll run a bit with the line to test the integrity of the set. Then, if it's a good set, they'll just let you pull them over and hold still as you release the hook. I mean, 'really?' If you are going to be fishing for three days all day at the same river, plus, if you have the methodology down and you are catching large fish over and over again – s0metimes maybe even the same fish – you are probably going to get bored. You may say, *'Not me - Never!*, but you probably will.

When this happens to me, I pull my head up off the river and I take a look around. In this case, on the San Juan below Navajo dam, you have a great opportunity at hand. The banks of the San Juan River are bound by sandstone cliffs lined with huge cottonwood trees. Huge books of rock are broken off to make hidden nooks and arches in the cliffs. The cottonwood trees and willows along the bank give way to piñon, juniper, sage, and cactus at higher ledges with scattered Ponderosa pine and Douglas fir along the canyon rim. In some places, water from the smaller intermittent streams flow from secondary canyons that breach the sides of the San Juan River Canyon to make lush, overgrown riparian niches full of animal tracks.

Of particular interest to visitors in this area is Simon's Canyon. You can hike a mild-grade trail up the canyon between huge boulders on level sandstone ledges between Ponderosa and cedar trees to follow a natural footpath that leads on a self-guided tour with information plaques up to ancient Indian ruins dated to 1754.

Simon's Canyon.

The Simon Canyon Ruin is a small, one-room adobe-brick building built on top of a huge, isolated 20-foot tall boulder. The ruin is unique in that it is north of the San Juan River, which traditionally formed the border between the Navajo and the Utes making it the northwestern most extent of this clan of Navajo Indians.

The ancient people used a notched log to reach hand-tooled holes dug into the side of the boulder for fingers and toes to grab in climbing the rest of the way up the boulder to reach the adobe brick ruin. The notched log was then pulled up behind them to prevent enemies from climbing up behind them. A local spring as well as the stream below provided water. The canyon also contains remnants of an earlier human occupation. The view overlooking Simon Canyon is awesome along the entire hike. Simon Canyon itself has a sandy bottom with intermittent water flow, huge cottonwood trees- a natural wildlife game trail below the sandstone cliffs. The atmosphere of this place simply compels one's imagination to feel a natural sense of having arrived – this is a good place to make a stronghold for a clan to stay for a while.

The ruins at Simon's Canyon.

The Simon Canyon hike is the kind of local diversion that helps create a more memorable experience for me - especially if it is located at a venue that I frequently fish, or, if we have been driving, camping, fishing for a few days, such as over a week long road trip fishing multiple rivers in southwestern Colorado and New Mexico. Besides, a morning hike with the dogs is one of the best ways to enjoy a road trip and makes the dogs a lot more controllable and less energetic on the river for fishing later in the morning.

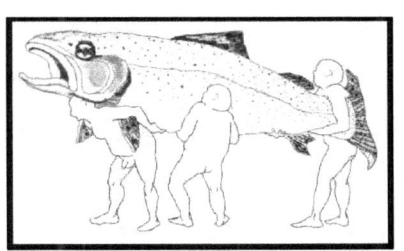

18. One of Those Days (by Al Marlowe)

"When someone tells you they would like to have a trout for dinner, consider the opportunity to be your destiny."

The day begins with a touch of expectation. You're going fishin'. Last night's forecast said it would be in the 70's, sunny and no wind. You're just finishing tying a Hare's Ear fly as your buddy rings the doorbell, causing your Golden (retriever) to bark in anticipation of having someone to throw a tennis ball for him. You throw your equipment in the back of his pickup and leave. Your Golden pouts when he learns he must stay home today.

On the way, the two of you talk about the weather, the economy, best flies to use, how the old truck is running, your wives, old girl friends, the Denver Nuggets basketball blown game, a new rod you need, future fishing trips, Saturday night's party, the new secretary at the office (a 23-year whose presence graces the atmosphere), the pain in your left shoulder and how it affects casting, and a few other topics. By the time the truck pulls into the parking area, all the world's problems have been solved, or at least discussed.

As the two of you rig your fly rods, your buddy suggests beginning with a Blue Wing Olive.

"*With the sun on the water like this*," he says, "*the baetis hatch should come off pretty soon.*"

You disagree and tie on a caddis larva imitation. The water is very clear and already, a few fish are rising.

Both of you struggle into neoprene waders and wonder if they're going to be too hot today. You put on your vest filled with seven fly boxes, 23 leaders, tippet material, thermometer, insect seine, vials for insect and nymph specimens (to tie better imitations at home), insect repellant, toilet paper, sun screen, fly floatant, line dressing, forceps, spare glasses, and a sandwich left over from last month's trip. Just before slamming the truck door shut, you remember the camera. As you reach under the seat, you realize it's still on the table at home.

To avoid the sections of the river that get fished hard, you decide to hike the trail to a riffle, two miles downstream. After working up a sweat in those hot waders, you pause for a cool drink of water before fishing. You get into the stream and start casting. The fly lands with a splash, scattering several small brookies and a 17-inch brown. You're a bit rusty, not having picked up a fly-rod since last year.

You move on to the next pool, hoping your casting improves. A fish is rising at the tail of a small riffle. Ignoring the canopy of tree branches overhead, you begin false casting. Just as you begin the final cast, your rod stops sharply, the fly hung in the trees. By the time the leader is repaired and a new fly tied on, the fish is no longer rising.

Moving on upstream to the deep run opposite the point bar, you wade into the water and discover the beavers have been very busy. The discovery is made when you find a channel they have deepened. You discover it by falling in over your waders. At least the day is warm and the wet and the resultant moist slimy feeling in your waders is cooling.

You crawl out on the bank and remove the neoprene waders. The warm sun soon has your jeans dry. Before getting back into your waders, you decide to fill the vacancy in your stomach. The first sandwich you get out of the tattered vest is the moldy ham and cheese, left from an earlier venture. You break it into several pieces for the chipmunks that have come to you begging for anything you can spare and pull out the other sandwich. Your wife has lovingly made a fresh lunch this morning. It's corned beef on rye with cheddar cheese, Grey Poupon mustard, lettuce, sprouts and a couple of dill pickles and chips. After pouring the water out of the water-proof bag, you feed this wet morsel to the chipmunks, as well. At least the pickles are still ok.

The sun has warmed the day. The temperature is quite pleasant. The next place you fish is a slow stretch the beavers have enlarged with a dam. Next to an undercut bank, a fish has been rising at one minute intervals, taking tiny duns. Your buddy was right. They are taking baetis adults.

Since you were rigged for nymphs, you now must change your leader. You switch to one of 10 feet, tapered to 6x. You tie on a No. 20 Blue Wing Olive, one you bought in a shop for $1.45. After five casts, a 15-inch rainbow takes it. The hook is set and the line promptly goes slack as the poorly tied knot pulls loose.

You remember that the day started by your wife suggesting she sure would like to have trout for supper. By mid-afternoon, you have caught three fish. The one you kept is 9 inches. You keep flailing the water, hoping for two or three more. Four fish would make a meal. Even if they are only 9-inchers.

About 30 minutes later, the baetis hatch has finished. You go back to nymphs. Fortunately, by now the thinner tail of the new leader has been clipped and snapped off to the point the remainder of the line is thick enough for a heavier fly. The first one tied on is a girdle bug, a stonefly or some other imitation. It is to be fished deep with weight. After three casts, the line stops. It's not a fish, though. It's snagged on the bottom. After a few tugs, the line goes slack and you retrieve an even shorter leader sans fly.

The sun is low in the west. You still have one fish in your creel. Your wife still wants a fish dinner. Surface activity has stopped and no interest has been shown in your nymph for over an hour. You meet your buddy back at the truck.

You throw your equipment in the back of his pickup and leave. On the way home, the two of you talk about the weather, the economy, best flies to use, how the old truck is running, your wives, old girl friends, the Nuggets blown game, a new rod you need, future fishing trips, Saturday night's party, the new secretary at the office (the 23-year old in the office), the pain in your left shoulder and how it affects casting, and a few other topics. By the time the truck pulls into the driveway, all the world's problems have been solved again, or at least discussed.

You open the front door. Your Golden has a tennis ball in his mouth, hoping you'll play with him. Your wife gives you a kiss and asks about your day. "*Great,*" you reply. "*It's just one of those days, one of those great days.*"

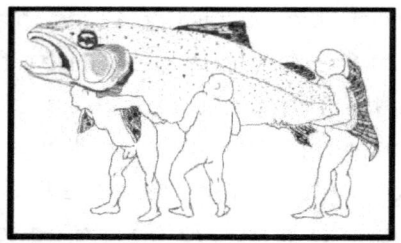

19. Ride Through the Clouds (by Al Marlowe)

"Wyoming's Cloud Peak Wilderness"

Cross Creek was glass clear. Rocks on the bottom, two feet below the surface, appeared to be only inches away. A few feet upstream, the water's surface was disturbed and a tiny insect became a trout's dessert. In seconds, the evidence was gone. The stream again flowed smooth and serene in the Cloud Peak Wilderness.

Along the trail to Highland Park, horse shoe prints had started to fade. Equine calling cards scattered on the ground were dry. Horses had not been on the trail since the previous autumn, causing the riders to wonder if snow might perhaps block their progress at the higher passes. In a few spots, the trail led down steep grades. Loose rock caused the rider to consider the consequences of a slip. The horse was unconcerned, seeming to say, *'This is nothing, Boss. I've seen worse.'*

Named for the highest peak in the Bighorn Mountains, the Cloud Peak Wilderness Area was established in 1932, and was first managed as a Primitive Area by the Forest Service. Cloud Peak, 13,175 feet high, is located near the center of the 300 square mile wilderness. It is drained in all directions by countless creeks and streams. Its glacially carved hanging valleys are dotted with innumerable clear alpine lakes. Dense pine forests, boulder fields, and large open parks predominate in a landscape punctuated with high barren peaks.

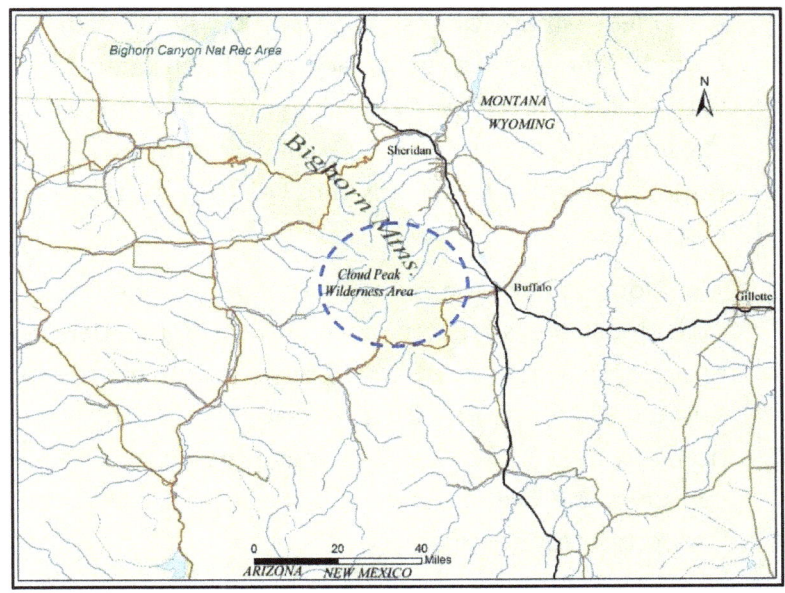

Location of Cloud Peak Wilderness Area, Wyoming.

Here, the landscape is rugged. It is young, geologically. Scattered remnants of once massive glaciers still cling to the mountains on north- and east-facing slopes. Along valleys, gouged out by mile-thick ice at the close of the Pleistocene, moraines, sinuous ribbons of granite boulders, bear silent witness to where the glaciers finished their work.

Timberline is low in the Bighorns, scarcely more than 10,000 feet to perhaps 10,500. Alpine meadows extend for miles in places. In July of '91, they were covered with countless forms of wildflowers in blue, red, yellow, white, and all shades in between. Paintbrush in yellow, red, and a magenta that's almost fluorescent sprout from the earth in seemingly unlikely places. Alpine forget-me-nots with brilliant, tiny blue petals cover the high meadows, causing one to be careful about stepping off a trail. Bright pink alpine laurel blossoms line the moist banks of high lakes.

The Cloud Peak Wilderness has an extensive network of trails. Most are suited to horse travel. With adequate provisions, a traveler could wander for weeks, as did Bridger, Colter, and others, seeing few if any other humans. It would be easy to transport oneself back a century and a half to share the same vistas the Sioux and Cheyenne called home.

The Hunter Corrals trailhead is recommended by the Forest Service for horse travelers. It has holding pens and loading ramps for horses and parking for horse trailers and vehicles. The corrals give access to several trails heading into the Cloud Peak Wilderness. Hunter Corrals is about 12 miles west from the town of Buffalo and a mile off U. S. 16.

The Solitude Trail heads at the Corrals and is one of the more popular rides. It makes a loop that takes the rider through the heart of the wilderness in a distance of about 70 miles. Plan about a week on this ride. Ten days would be even better.

The trail heads west from the Corrals, crossing the wilderness boundary after about five miles. Two miles further, at Soldier Park, the trail divides. The fork to the right takes you past Elk Lake, Frying Pan Lake, just off the main trail, and around Willow Park Reservoir. From there, you'll follow Kearny Creek on the way to Highland Park, a square mile of flat, lush, green meadow in an alpine setting.

After leaving the Park, the trail crosses three easy passes on the way to the northern boundary of the wilderness. It soon connects with the East Fork of Big Goose Creek, which leads south to Lake Geneva and over Geneva Pass. Eventually, you'll arrive at Lake Solitude, set at the bottom of a steep-walled valley in the shadow of 11,321-foot Elk Mountain. The trail is now heading east toward Florence Pass, the high point of the ride at 10,800 feet. From the pass, it's all downhill through a long, nearly flat, outwash plain, where the trail winds its way in and out of the trees on the way to Soldier Park and the Corrals.

There are several campgrounds along the trail, although it isn't required that they be used. In some of the more heavily used sites, gathering firewood may be a chore as the easy to get wood is gone.

From many sections of the trail, Cloud Peak and its nearby neighbor, Black Tooth Mountain, are visible, serving as prominent landmarks. Several square miles around Cloud Peak are covered with lakes. Anglers will need to carry fishing tackle. A nine-foot, four-piece fly rod in weight five or six will work just fine. A weight forward line will make long casts on the windy lakes a bit easier.

Spin fishermen should take an assortment of lures like Mepps, Panther Martin, and Rooster Tail spinners as well as an assortment of spoons. Bait is legal to use on the many rainbow, brook, and cutthroat trout but the fish are so eager to hit a lure, worms are almost too much trouble.

Be sure to pack a camera in your saddle bag. The scenery is cooperative, posing without complaint, even with the slowest shutter speed. A clear day in the Cloud Peak Wilderness will likely offer the photographer a rare chance to capture the sky at its best.

Deer, elk, and moose are seen frequently in the wilderness. Be cautious around moose as they are unpredictable. They're big enough that they don't have to yield the right of way.

There are other trails beside Solitude that will make for shorter rides. All will take the rider into some of the finest scenery in the Bighorn Mountains. A mile or so past the wilderness boundary, along the Solitude Trail, a trail leads south to the Seven Brothers Lakes. Return by way of Buffalo Park, back to the corrals. A campground at the lakes makes this 12-mile ride ideal for an overnighter.

Circle Park Campground, about three miles south of Hunter Corrals and three miles west of U. S. 16, could be the starting place for a two or three-day trip into the South Fork Ponds area. The glacially carved cirques of Big Horn Peak, about five miles to the west, can be seen from the ponds. It will be necessary to park your rig and unload the horses along the road to the east as horses are not permitted in the campground.

Several outfitters serve the Cloud Peak area. Most offer pack trips and guided hunts in the fall. A couple of them have guest facilities. Whether you use an outfitter or plan a do-it-yourself ride, the Cloud Peak Wilderness will be a memorable experience.

It's been a long ride. Meals prepared on open fires tasted better than the same foods when cooked at home. The views are remembered, clear streams meander through the mind. Sore muscles and stiff legs make the riders long for a refreshing shower and perhaps a hot tub. Even as gear is being loaded for the trip home, rider's thoughts are of returning to the Cloud Peak Wilderness.

Access - The Cloud Peak Wilderness is located in Bighorn, Johnson and Sheridan Counties in Northern Wyoming, within the Bighorn National Forest. It lies west of I-90 between the cities of Buffalo and Sheridan. It is bounded on the west by U. S 20, U. S. 14 on the north, and U. S. 16 on the south.

Forest Service roads access the wilderness trails. Not all are open to the public because landowners lock the gates. Consult a NF map concerning road closures or contact the Forest Supervisor, Bighorn National Forest, 1969 S. Sheridan Ave., Sheridan WY 82801.

Entrance to the Could Peak Wilderness requires a permit. The registration form can be completed beforehand online.

Special Regulations apply to accessing the Cloud Peak Wilderness area related to use of vehicles, campfires, collecting wood, campsites, care and keeping of stock animals, trash, etc.

Hunting is only allowed through certified outfitters.

About 20 NF campgrounds surround the wilderness. Be aware that horses are prohibited within the campgrounds. Check with the Forest Supervisor for information on parking horse trailers and vehicles.

Details as to point of entry trails are viewable online.

Climate - Wind is the one condition that is a constant. One Wyoming resident said, "*It doesn't always blow this way, sometimes it comes from the opposite direction.*" Even though the wilderness is usually breezy, it's not unpleasant.

Because of the Northwest to Southeast orientation of the mountain range, storms can sneak in with little warning. Be prepared for anything, even snow in mid-summer. Usually, though, summer weather will be pleasant with a late afternoon shower.

One thing that will be noticed is the extreme clarity of the air. The sky appears to be a darker blue, the clouds whiter. With sparse industrial commerce in Wyoming, there few sources of atmospheric contribution from refineries or mills in the area.

July and August are good times for horse riders to visit Cloud Peak Wilderness. What snow remains will rarely block access except on the higher trails. Day time temperatures range from the 40s to the 60s. The higher you ride, the cooler the temperatures you will encounter.

Wilderness Camping - Campsites in the wilderness must be kept at least 100 feet from any water source. Human waste and trash must be packed out. When breaking camp, try to hide any traces of your visit.

Horses - The Forest Service suggests using the least number of horses. No more than 15 horses may be used by any one group. Free pamphlets with additional information are available from the Forest Supervisor.

Wildlife - The wilderness is home to many species of song birds and small animals like chipmunks, ground squirrels, and marmots. Deer, elk, and moose are common. Black bears inhabit the area. Your sleeping and cooking areas should be separated to discourage Bruin from prowling through your camp.

Other Services - Gas, groceries, and meals are available at most of the towns serving the area. Fishing licenses are readily available in some surprisingly out of the way places. Emergency medical services and veterinary clinics are available in Sheridan, Buffalo, Worland, Lovell, and Graybull.

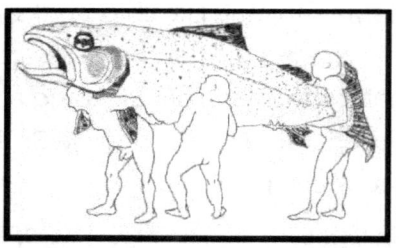

20. Al's Designer Humpy (by Al Marlowe)

"Nobody should love your special humpy more than a fat trout."

For many years, the Humpy has proven itself a good fly to use on fast streams, especially those in the mountain states of the west. The pattern usually is tied with natural colors of elk- or deer-hair. My experience of the past few years has shown me its versatility can be expanded by using various colors of dyed hair, hackle and other materials. Improvements in dying technology have made it possible to design the Humpy as a hatch matching pattern, making it an important addition to the fisherman's fly box.

Since the Humpy uses deer- or elk-hair, which is hollow, it has excellent floating qualities. New technology makes possible the art of dying deer- and elk-hair without making it stiff or brittle. In my tying materials, I have pieces of hair dyed olive-green, rust, black, light- and dark-brown and some colors I can't name or pronounce.

Green hair makes a high-floating Green Drake imitation. Tied with light-brown hair, I have used it during a Quill Gordon hatch. Using black elk-hair, I tied Humpies that proved to be excellent Grey Drake imitations, taking many brookies on a high-mountain stream several summers ago during a Grey Drake hatch.

The idea of using the Humpy as a hatch matcher may have originated in New Zealand according to Jack Dennis, of Jackson, Wyoming. Jack operates an outdoor shop and is a well-known fly tier. The pattern is very popular down under because the streams are large and fast, making a highly visible, high floating fly necessary. The Humpy has also been used in an Adams pattern to imitate the baetis mayflies of Hebgen Lake near Yellowstone National Park. I first learned of using the Humpy as a hatch matching fly at a tying seminar Jack conducted in Denver in 1985.

When fishing the Designer Humpy, I use it like I would any hatch matching pattern. My experience has convinced me that an exact imitation, one having eyelashes, teeth and under-wing hair, is not needed in most cases. With the exception of a few streams which are subjected to heavy fishing pressure, like the Cheeseman Canyon section of the South Platte River of Colorado, a fly in the correct size and color that suggests the natural insect will take fish. For this situation, the Humpy, in appropriate color and size, works very well.

Close-up of Al's Designer Humpy.

The Humpy's buoyancy makes it especially useful in fast currents as it rides without sinking. I usually treat my flies with floatant, but that is not needed for the Humpy. An ideal place to us a Humpy is the head of a pool where the current is fastest. Put the fly just above the pool, then let it drift into the deeper, slower water. Expect a strike before the fly is out of the fast water. I prefer to cast perpendicular to the current rather than upstream. This allows me to maintain a tight line, reduces slack and assists setting the hook on a strike.

The Humpy is a bulky fly except in sizes smaller than No. 16. The fisherman will find the fly easier to cast by matching the leader tippet to the fly size. Casting a No. 10 or 12 Humpy with a 7x tippet results in a cast that will not straighten the leader, causing the fly to fall on the water in a fish frightening splash. A 3x leader tippet will handle the Humpy in sizes 10 through 14. For smaller fly sizes use a 4x or 5x tippet. Remember that both tippet and hook sizes get smaller as the size number gets larger.

I have found only one problem with the Humpy, the fly is tied with hair and eventually, the trout's sharp teeth will cut it. This problem is remedied to a degree by using soft hair which is more resistant to the trout's teeth. However, the ragged appearance of a well-used fly doesn't hinder its performance. The fish take a torn and tattered Humpy as eagerly as one fresh from the tiers vise.

The Humpy also works best tied with soft deer- or elk-hair, both for its floating qualities and tying ease. Previously, the only way to vary the color of the Humpy was to use darker or lighter hair. The problem with this is that dark hair often has undesirable traits that affect durability. A few years ago, Rocky Mountain Dubbing Co. of Riverton, Wyoming developed a method of dying elk- and deer-hair without causing it to become brittle or stiff, retaining the hair's natural flexibility while the hide remained pliable. This technology has made it possible to unite the high floating qualities of the Humpy with various colors of hair and hackle to tie a fly to match a hatch.

Be extremely selective when purchasing elk- or deer-hair for tying the Humpy. Reject any hair that is from the spinal area or the rump of the hide. The best hair will be found on the sides and flanks. For tying the smaller sizes (smaller than 14 or 16) the fine hair from the front legs is excellent. Since most tiers will buy patches of hair rather than an entire hide, make your selections based on the sizes you will tie. Purchase hair in several diameters. If the hair has become brittle or the skin stiff or hard from dying, don't waste your money on it.

For tying most flies, I use Mustad hooks. However, when tying the Humpy in size 10 or 12, I prefer the Tiemco hooks because of their slightly better shape in the bend. This makes it a little easier to tie a well-proportioned fly. The Mustad hook is fine for the Humpy in sizes smaller than No. 12. Correct proportions are important for tying the Humpy in order to have it float properly. If the tail is too short or the wings too high, it will tend to float on its side or head.

The Humpy is useful in all sizes commonly used for dry flies, from No. 8 to as small as No. 22. The size (diameter) and amount of hair used should be proportional to the hook size. In other words, don't try to tie a size 18 Humpy with a fistful of very coarse hair. With experience will come the ability to judge the amount of hair to use on any particular hook size. If a quantity of hair is difficult to tie properly, you have likely used too much.

Tie your Designer Humpy as follows;

1- Begin by securing the thread at the mid-point of the hook shank. This is a reference point for several steps in tying the fly. If the thread is started forward of the mid-point, insufficient room will be left for the head.

2- The tail hair should equal the hook length and be tied in at the mid-point of the hook shank. The tips of the hair should be even and the butts trimmed to correct length. I like to use moose hair for the tail because it resists flaring, allowing the fly to float properly. Apply a small amount of cement to the wraps. My preference is a cement that penetrates rather than one that builds up on the surface.

3- The body hair is trimmed to equal the length from the hook eye to the tip of the tai. Tie in the butt-end at the mid-point of the hook. This allows sufficient length to form the wings after making the hump. The tips of the body hair should be evened by using a hair stacker. Trim the butts even. Soft elk- or deer-hair will flair considerably, a desirable quality in making a well formed body.

4- Tie in the body hair at the mid-point. Make the first wrap snug, with sufficient tension to not slip, followed by two or three successively tighter wraps. Then, wrap the thread evenly and tightly back to the bend of the hook. Apply cement lightly.

5- To make the fly look more buggy, tie in peacock herl or dubbing of appropriate color and wrap forward to the mid-point. For flies in size 16 or smaller, one strand of herl is enough. Avoid making the underbody so bulky the gape will have inadequate hooking ability. Secure and remove excess material.

6- Bring the body hair forward and secure at the mid-point, with several wraps. As you bring the hair forward, twist it very slightly. This will prevent rotation of the hair around the hook shank. A space of about one millimeter is needed between the body and wing to make room for winding the hackle.

7- Raise the hair to a 90-degree angle. Then bring the thread forward and build up a wedge to hold the hair upright.

8- Divide the upright hair to form the wings and separate them with X-wraps.

9- After making the X-wraps, bring the thread in front of the wings. Make several wraps around the base of each wing. Wrap the thread in a counter-clock-wise direction around the right wing (as seen from the front). Finish the wraps with the thread behind the wing and tighten, using sufficient tension to hold the wing at a 35 to 40-degree angle from vertical. Make one or two wraps and bring the thread forward of the wings. Repeat the procedure on the left wing in a clock-wise direction. This will give better definition to the wings, enhancing the appearance of the finished fly. The two wings should be separated by about 70 to 80 degrees (eyeballing the angle will be accurate enough).

10- Tie in two hackles. Since the Humpy is designed for fast water, only top quality hackle should be used. Before trimming the hackle butts, build up a base of thread as illustrated. This makes a smooth transition for the hackle wraps from behind to forward of the wing. Apply cement lightly and make two or three wraps behind the wing and two or three more in front.

11- Whip-finish and cement the head.

12- A line from the tip of the tail to the top of the wing should form a 45-degree angle. By using these proportions, the finished fly will float properly.

13- Tie your fresh Designer Humpy to a leader tippet and catch fish.

Tying the Humpy is time intensive but not difficult. Just be patient and keep at it until you are satisfied with the results. If you learn to tie the Humpy properly and with correct proportions, other patterns will be extremely easy to tie.

The variations possible for tying the Designer Humpy are almost without limit. Let your imagination be your inspiration. If you have extraordinary eyesight and exceptional patience, tie some in small sizes like Nos. 22 or 24. When tying this fly in the smaller sizes, it will be necessary to use finer hair and less of it to get the proportions correct. For flies in sizes 8 or 10 and down to

14 or 16 use peacock herl for the underbody to produce a buggy look. Another useful underbody material is antron-blend dubbing in a color appropriate to the rest of the fly. The antron gives a lifelike sparkle to the fly. Other possible variations include assorted wing materials like antron yarn, poly yarn or calf-hair. The wings can be tied upright-divided or Trude style, which is tied in at a 45-degree angle in front of the body.

I have come to rely on the Humpy as my main fly. Its buoyancy makes it float well in the fast water I enjoy fishing. In the larger sizes, it is highly visible, making it easy to follow in the current. This is appreciated by those of us no longer possessing 20/20 vision. Most important of all, it appeals to the fish. By tying the Designer Humpy in various colors, it will imitate many of the insects trout feed on, making it a useful addition to your fly box.

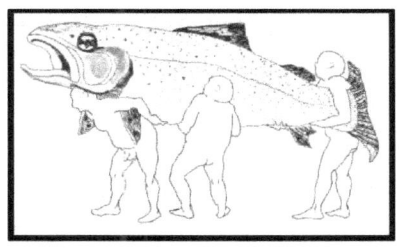

21. Fishing the "Un-hatches" (by Al Marlowe)

"When summer hatches aren't hatching during your visit to the river..."

The Salmon Fly, March Brown, and Green Drake hatches offer exceptional summer fly fishing. When the duns are on the water, trout abandon their instinctive caution and recklessly attack a well-presented imitation. The problem is the hatches don't last long enough. Even at their peak, the adult insects are around only a few weeks. Mayflies – Green Drakes, Callibaetis, or Tricos – that hang around as long as a month or two, usually appear for only a few hours each day. That is, providing conditions are ideal. If the weather is uncooperative, they may even be no-shows. What's the solution? When the insects don't hatch, fish the un-hatches.

So what is an un-hatch? A look beneath the surface of our streams and lakes will reveal myriad life forms that rarely or never appear on top. These abundant species constitute a significant portion of the biomass in our rivers, lakes and ponds. Though nymphs supply a trout with up to 90-percent of its diet, other organisms are also important. This means that imitations of crustaceans, worms, leeches, and many other aquatic critters can be effectively fished throughout most of the year.

Un-hatches also include insects that get into the water by accident. Grasshoppers, ants and beetles are frequently victims of an errant breeze that turns them into instant fish food. During the spring when rainbows are spawning, many an egg ends up feeding a hungry fish. In short, un-hatches are what keeps a trout's belly full when the Light Hendricksons, Yellow Stones and Green Caddis are not around.

One of the most widely available un-hatches is a crustacean, the scud. Three families and about 90 species are found in North America. Mature scuds vary in length from less than a quarter-inch to nearly one inch. They are abundant in both streams and still-waters, making them an important food source throughout the year. Scuds come in a spectrum of bright colors from green, tan, gray, pink, or white to shades in between. Each location will often have a color that produces best. On a number of Western rivers, a dirty-yellow or burnt-orange scud takes trout when other colors bring only yawns from bored fish. Mahogany-brown attracts hungry trout on Utah's Green River.

Where ever you fish the scud, stock your fly box with a spectrum of colors and sizes. If one is unproductive, perhaps another will work. Tail-waters are especially good places to fish a scud as there are usually quite a few that make their way from the reservoir into the stream. Fish it with a dead drift. Use weight on the leader rather than on the fly to allow it to tumble freely in the current.

In a lake or pond, look for scuds in weed beds and debris in the shallow water near shore. Observing them there will yield clues on how to fish imitations. Near weed beds is a good place to use them. Retrieve the scud with short jerks to duplicate their energetic swimming motion.

Like scuds, earthworms are also abundant. There are estimated to be more than 200 species in North America, many being found in aquatic environments. While it may have been named for New Mexico's famed trout stream, the San Juan Worm is just as effective on other rivers. Like the scud, these small worms - one-quarter to two inches in length - come in a variety of brilliant colors. Easy to imitate, the fly usually consists of nothing more than a strip of Ultra Chenille tied to a hook. While red is the most popular color, burnt-orange, light-brown, and purple imitations also work well. The worm is helpless in a current so fish it with a dead-drift.

Speaking of worms, anglers should not overlook leeches. Ranging in length from less than one-half inch to a foot or more, these variously colored, flat-bodied worms are found in a nearly all aquatic habitats. One of the more popular imitations is the Woolly Bugger. Favored colors are olive, black, brown, and purple in large sizes, Nos. 2 through 12. It is equally effective in lakes, ponds or streams.

In a lake, Woolly Buggers are especially effective when fished from a belly boat on a sinking line. A leech moves by attaching its forward sucker to the bottom or to weeds, contracting its body, and then attaching the rear sucker. Its motion is similar when swimming. Twitch the rod tip or retrieve the line in short jerks to duplicate the slow undulations of a leech. It should be fished deep, on the bottom, so it may also be necessary to weight the hook when tying it. Be prepared to have the line suddenly ripped from your hand as a heavy fish tries to swim away with your fly.

Perfect your roll cast for fishing the lake shoreline. Throwing a heavy Woolly Bugger with a conventional cast is a good way to hit yourself in the head, especially on a windy day.

In a stream, fish it with a dead drift, using just enough weight to get the leech near the bottom. Though effective in deep runs, don't overlook slow back-waters near the bank. Strip line in short jerks to make the marabou tail come alive. Other good patterns are the Chamois and Bunny Leeches

Trout anglers have two additional opportunities to fish the un-hatches. Each spring, rainbows and cutthroats give in to natural urges to reproduce, as do browns and brookies in the fall. When a female lays her eggs on a redd, other fish wait nearby to gobble up any that drift away. A yarn egg is the fly to use at spawning time. It works in deep runs and shallow riffles. It works on browns, brookies, rainbows and cutthroats. The fly is simple, a short piece of fluorescent pink, red, orange, or yellow polypropylene yarn tightly tied on a hook so that it flares into a ball. During the brief period of spawning activity, the egg will take lots of trout. Fish it dead drift near the bottom.

Summer brings trout a cornucopia of delectable morsels in the form of ants, beetles, hoppers, spiders, and cicadas. These and other terrestrial insects become available as a result of wind or some other mishap that deposits them in the water where cruising trout await such morsels. Their ensuing struggle to escape has an effect somewhat like ringing the dinner bell for a starving brown. Fish terrestrials close to the bank. If a hit doesn't occur immediately, retrieve it with short twitches and jerks to impart the appearance of a struggling insect. Then hang onto your rod.

A graphite fly rod and a single-action reel having a smooth drag are preferred for fishing the un-hatches. The rod should have enough backbone to handle weighted flies as well as bulky, wind resistant terrestrial patterns. A nine-foot, four- to six-weight is a good choice.

On streams, a floating line will do just fine. If fish are finicky feeders, try a tapered leader with a fine tippet, especially when using small patterns in clear water. Otherwise, three to six feet of 3X or 4X material will work. Weight the leader a foot or so above the fly. Use enough to get the fly down but not so much that it snags frequently. A strike indicator combined with the short-line technique will help detect takes when hits are subtle. As with nymph fishing, the angler will often be drifting a fly close to visible fish. Eight to ten feet of line plus the leader is plenty. Set the hook any time the indicator hesitates or moves in the wrong direction, such as upstream. It may be just a snag. Then again, it could be a wall hanger.

On lakes, a fast-sinking line is the best choice for fishing leeches and scuds. To find the best depth, start counting when the fly hits the water, then start the retrieve. Determine the count that places the fly near the bottom. When fish are located, continue working your fly at that depth.

Terrestrials like beetles, hoppers and ants should be fished dry with a floating line. Casting into brush along the bank and pulling the fly so that it falls on the water with a "plop" can be very effective. Whether on a stream or lake, give 'em some action so they look alive.

There are numerous un-hatch flies that can be effective in addition to these. Patterns that imitate bait fish, frogs, crayfish, spiders, cicadas, and even mice can be effective. Each should be fished with an action appropriate to the pattern.

Taking a 17-inch trout that has risen to a dry-fly tied by the angler is one of summer's great pleasures. Lots of hungry trout taking hordes of mayflies in showy rises is what dry-fly fishing is about. Unfortunately, neither summer nor the hatches last long enough. For that time of day or season when surface activity is slow, the fly-rodder who fishes the un-hatches will enjoy action throughout the year.

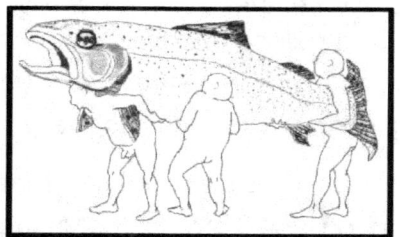

22. The Flat Tops Wilderness, Colorado (by Al Marlowe)

"An Angler's Paradise"

The Flat Tops, located in west-central Colorado in the White River National Forest, is a unique place. It is unlike any other mountain range in the state. There are no tall spires, no fourteeners. Rather, it is a high plateau, appearing as a massive block of rock, pushed upward by some giant's hand, and planed level.

On its surface, covering several hundred square miles, long extinct volcanic vents are filled with water. In other places, glaciers have gouged deep valleys and plowed debris into ridges, damming streams.

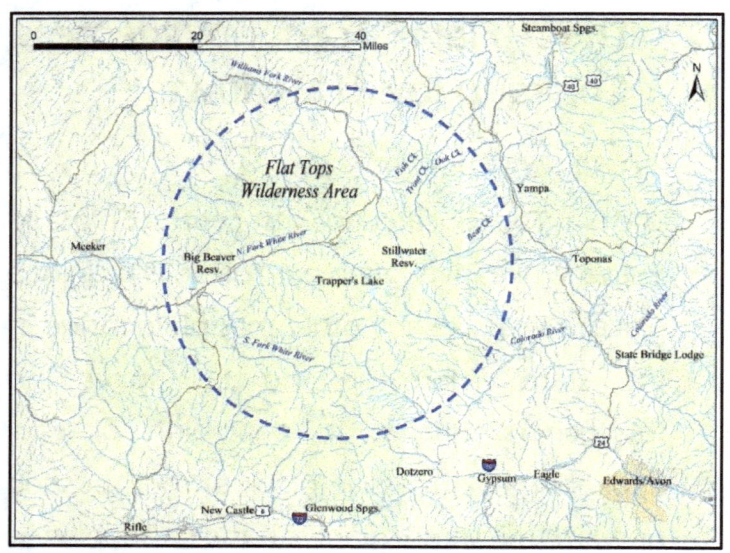

Location of abundant fishing venues in Flat Tops Wilderness Area, Colorado.

Because of its location, the Flat Tops collects an abundance of precipitation. Water, collected by lakes and drained by streams, makes the region an angler's paradise. Names like Derby, Grizzly, Sweetwater, Canyon, Doe, Fawn, Buck, and Spring creeks pop up all over the map. There's Star Lake, Wall, Keener, Oyster, Shepherd and others, causing the angler to conjure visions of large, hungry trout.

There's something for fishermen of all persuasions. Fly casters have a choice of streams, from small creeks and beaver ponds to rivers hiding fish of surprising proportions. Lakes and ponds beckon to the spinner fisherman. Some have big surprises. If you should try the

Mandall lakes, hang onto your rod. That submerged log you thought you snagged just may turn out to be a ten-pound mackinaw.

Author and Melvin enjoying a beaver pond.

So where should one begin in a quest for angling adventure in this most magnificent wilderness? To cover each place would require a book. Let's examine a few waters, though, that will allow an angler to use a favorite method.

As you head west on I-70 after passing the towns of Eagle and Gypsum, jump off at Dotsero and follow the Colorado upstream for a couple of miles to Deep Creek. The creek runs fast as it plunges and wends its way to the Colorado. For the first mile along the gravel road, the water is private. In another mile, the road departs the creek. It's a small stream in a half-mile deep canyon but in the dozen miles below Deep Lake, it's reported to have brooks, rainbows and few fishermen.

The rough gravel path continues on another 37 miles before ending beside the South Fork of the White River. On the way along the Coffee Pot Road, Deep Lake will tempt the angler to stop off early. Being an extinct volcanic crater, the lake lives up to its name. Its waters hold brook trout and mackinaws. In 1949, a state record mac was taken here, 42 inches long and 36 pounds.

After another eight miles, you'll come to The Meadows. Parking at the trailhead gives access to the upper part of the South Fork. It's a small stream, having mostly brookies. Except in late summer, anglers will find few rising fish. But drifting a No. 12 or 14 Humpy will attract strikes from ravenous trout.

Downstream, the South Fork is larger and faster as it flows toward the South Fork Campground. In between, there's more than a dozen miles of wilderness water. The cutthroats and rainbows are bigger than the brookies above but just as impatient to take a fly or spinner.

Along the north side of the Flat Tops, go east out of Meeker on Rio Blanco County Road 8. Near Avery Lake, the South and North forks blend their waters. Continuing east from Avery takes you along the North Fork of the White. Being easier to reach, it gets fished more than the South. By carefully studying your White

River National Forest map, though, you'll be able to find a few out of the way stretches of public water that hold brookies, browns, rainbows and cutthroats, all eager to take your Humpy or Elk Hair Caddis.

A few miles east of Buford, detour south to Marvine Creek. It's small as are many of its fish. But not all. Lurking in some of the clear, deep pools, sulking forms of twelve-inch cutts and rainbows will be seen by anglers who carefully approach the water. A trail follows the creek for six miles to the two Marvine Lakes. The upper has brookies of 12 inches or so. Cutthroats and brookies are taken in the lower.

Continuing upstream along the North Fork takes you to Trappers, the best known lake on the Flat Tops, home to naturally reproducing cutthroat trout. To ignore the others nearby, though, means passing up many opportunities. Just a mile to the east lies Little Trappers. This 30-acre lake can be easily fished from shore for 12-inch cutts. It's not too far, though, to take a belly boat.

On the way to Little Trappers, you will pass a small lake, hidden in the trees. Deadfalls litter parts of the shoreline. A casual glance suggests barren water. Appearances can be deceiving, though. Coffin Lake is rumored to have cutts averaging 16 inches, with some to five pounds. Inducing a hit is the challenge.

Then there are places like Mirror Lake, a few miles north of Trappers. Hordes of brookies can be seen in the lake's clear water as they scour the surface in search of edibles. With a seemingly unlimited supply of fish, any method goes here. Just between us, though, this is an ideal place to introduce a friend to fly fishing. Which fly? Whatever you tie on, though a No. 12 Rio Grande King will be voraciously attacked by the little monsters.

CR8 continues east to Ripple Creek Pass. A half-mile west of the summit, a trail points north to Pagoda Peak. A mile south-west of the peak lies Pagoda Lake, a small tree-lined lake holding 12-inch brookies eager to take a fly or spinner. The four-mile walk is easy, making this a pleasant over-nighter for backpackers.

Mrs. Marlow and two goldens enjoying the fishing.

OK, so now that we have some ideas of places to fish, what do we use? In some cases, method is determined by regulation. In Trappers Lake, it's flies and lures only.

And since many of the fish caught will need to be returned because of size restrictions, it won't hurt to pinch down the barbs on flies and avoid the use of treble hooks on lures. Other waters allow the use of bait. When that's the case, worms, 'crawlers or grasshoppers can be hard to beat.

Hardware anglers will find a variety of lures that work. Rooster Tails having brown, yellow, and black, in some combination, in 1/16 and 1/8 ounce sizes are effective. Mepps and Panther Martins lures will also be productive spinners. Kastmasters, in silver, gold or silver/blue are proven fish-getters.

Fly casters have the greatest choice, especially those who are also tiers. Brook trout in lakes are attracted to brightly colored patterns like a Royal Coachman streamer in sizes 6 to 12. Spruce Fly streamers should also work. Use a sinking line to get the fly down deep and retrieve it with short twitches.

When fishing from a float tube or canoe, trolling one of these streamers is an easy way to fish. Also effective with this method are Woolly Buggers in green, black, or brown. Use a sinking line here, too.

For times when there's lots of rising fish, it will be hard to go wrong with a Humpy or an Elk Hair Caddis. Fish these in a size that approximates the naturals on the water. Be sure to include patterns like the Adams in your fly box, especially in small sizes. Lake fish seem to go for gray.

Sometimes those rising fish aren't taking adult insects. When that's the case, switch to a Hare's Ear nymph in an appropriate size and color; tan, brown or olive. If you tie your own, make the wing case with Crystal Hair or Crystal Flash to better imitate an emerging insect and fish it in the surface film.

Fishing the Flat Tops lakes usually means being there early. Ice out is the ideal time. Unfortunately, many of the lakes will be difficult to get to. It may require skis or snowshoes. The effort has its rewards, though; fewer people, more fish. Also bigger fish. Just a couple years ago, a kid took a five-pound brookie from Skinny Fish Lake in May.

Later in the season, when the snows have melted, the lakes will be most productive early and late in the day. As the sun creeps higher, the fish will retreat to deeper water, making them hard to reach from shore. A belly boat will pay off then.

Stream fishermen have just the opposite situation presented them. The White River, both forks, are at their peak flows early. But by mid-July, they're often running clear. Fly fishing begins to peak as the water flow declines. Warm sunny days bring out hordes of bugs, attracting fish. Mid-morning to late-afternoon seems to be the most productive time to be on the water. So what does this suggest? Try the lakes early and late in the day, spend the middle on a stream.

This is only a glance into fishing the Flat Tops. With its many streams and lakes, accessible by nearly 400 miles of trails, an angler would be hard pressed to do it all in a summer. Check the White River National Forest maps read through fishing guides. Pick out a few spots but save one special place for next season, because you will be compelled to return.

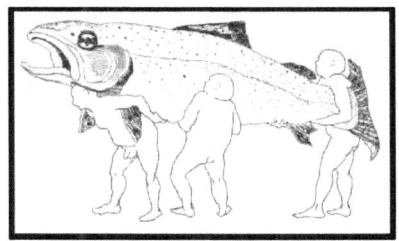

23. Fly Tying (by Al Marlowe)

"Sooner or later, all trout fishermen become fly tiers."

Most do it because of the cost of hand-tied flies. That's the reason I became a tier. I took up fly fishing shortly after settling in Colorado and learning that brookies will eagerly take a fly. Later, I even caught a couple of trout on a fly in small streams and beaver ponds.

When I took up fly fishing, a person could buy flies for fifteen cents or less if buying them by the dozen. Back then, there were almost no fly shops catering to anglers long on cash and short on time. Within the past few years, though, the yuppie fly fisherman arrived on the scene. Fly shops quickly sprang up to take their mon...– er, to serve them. Flies, now made by professional tiers that once sold for a quarter, suddenly required a second mortgage to purchase.

Prior to an angling excursion to the Frying Pan a few years back, I stopped in the Colorado Fly Fisher to restock my fly box. Ray Snapp, owner of the establishment in Lakewood, had gone fishing so Rhonda, Ray's wife and partner, helped me pick out a few patterns that afternoon.

"*How would you like to pay for these?*" Rhonda asked pleasantly. Rhonda always speaks pleasantly.

I stood staring at the cash register displaying the bill for my assortment of concoctions made of pheasant tail feathers, peacock herl, deer hair, and hackles. I tried to speak but a sudden tightness in my throat and strained breathing made it difficult to talk.

Rhonda responded quickly and started to dial 911 as soon as she observed the blue color in my face.

"*What are the choices?*" I asked after resting a few minutes.

"*Well, most of the doctors, attorneys, and insurance agents that come in here pay cash,*" she said, smiling and still speaking pleasantly. "*Of course, we do have an easy payment plan. Just fill out these papers.*"

Four hours later after filling out six forms and talking with two credit bureaus to explain why the credit report was incorrect, I left the store with my five dozen flies wondering how I would explain the $98.72 monthly payment spread out over five years to Jean (my wife). As I considered the money I had just spent, I realized I could fund an IRA for several years with one season's fly purchases. That's when I decided to tie my own flies.

A week later I returned to the Colorado Fly Fisher. This time, Rhonda had gone fishing and Ray minded the store. Ray is friendly but he doesn't smile as pleasantly as Rhonda. He's also not as good looking.

"*I've decided to take up fly tying,*" I said, "*what do I need?*"

"*Great,*" Ray said, smiling as he mentally added the dollars I would spend.

He led me to the display of vises and other tying tools.

"*Most beginners start out with this vise,*" Ray said, showing me a shiny model made in India. "*Of course, most eventually replace this inexpensive vise with one of better workmanship and quality. In the long run, you'll save money by getting the best.*"

He showed me Regal, API, and DynaKing vises, all selling close to the price of a used compact car. I decided on the Regal, the lowest priced model of the expensive vises.

Ray then showed me all the other tools I would need — tools I had no idea existed. There were thread bobbins, whip finishers, bodkins, scissors, hair stackers, hackle gauges, and a hundred other items to make tying easy. Half an hour later, the pile of tools resembled a small mountain.

I started to pull out my credit card to pay for the mound of tools when Ray stopped me. "*What patterns do you plan to tie?*" he asked.

That was something I hadn't considered so I mentally reviewed the contents of my fly boxes. The several containers held Pheasant Tails, Humpys, BWOs, Elk Hair Caddis, Halfbacks, Scuds, San Juan Worms, Woolly Buggers, and a hundred other patterns. Ray's eyes lit up like a slot machine at payoff when I told him what I wanted to tie. An hour later, the pile beside the register had grown in size and included hooks in all sizes and styles, Metz and Hoffman necks and saddles, deer, elk, and moose hair in a variety of natural and unnatural colors, chenille, floss, thread, foam, biots, Antron yarn, Larva Lace, Flashabou, Crystal Hair, and parts from countless birds, animals, and rodents.

"*How do you want to pay for this?*" Ray asked.

I stood staring at the cash register displaying the bill for my mountain of tools and materials. I tried to speak but a sudden tightness in my throat and strained breathing made it difficult to talk.

Ray responded quickly and started to dial 911 as soon as he observed the blue color in my face.

"*What are the choices?*" I asked after resting a few minutes.

"*Well, most of the doctors, attorneys, and insurance agents that come in here pay cash,*" Ray said. "*Of course, we do have an easy payment plan. Just fill out these papers.*"

Four hours later after filling out six forms and talking with two credit bureaus to explain why the credit report was still incorrect, I left the store with my fly tying stuff, wondering how to explain the $224.17 monthly payment spread out over five years to Jean. At least, I thought, now I can tie flies for twenty-five cents each.

At home, I unloaded the pickup and set my new purchase on the kitchen table. I clamped the vise to the table, placed a hook in the jaws and started to tie my first fly. It can't be too hard, I thought. I've watched Randy do this many times. Somehow, I managed to attach the materials for a Woolly Bugger to the hook, then began searching for the brown saddle I purchased to tie them. That's when I realized the dogs were no longer laying on the floor beside me.

Sunny and Spirit, our two golden retrievers, had gone outside to play. Spirit had a brown object in his mouth. Sunny had grabbed the other end of the brown object. *They really enjoy playing tug,'* I thought as I watched. I called the dogs. Spirit brought the remains of a fifty-dollar brown saddle to me. I decided to finish the fly with grizzly hackle.

A week later, I had succeeded in tying a total of five Woolly Buggers. I wanted to show Ray the results of my twenty-two hours at the vise.

"*Not bad,*" Ray said, trying to not discourage me. "*This something you thought up?*"

"*They're Woolly Buggers,*" I said.

"*Oh,*" Ray said.

He carefully examined the flies for several minutes.

"*Who taught you to tie?*" he asked.

Ray was very careful to conceal his amusement: "*Have you thought of taking lessons?*" he asked tactfully. "*We have a beginner's class starting in a couple of weeks.*"

"*Couldn't I learn from a book?*" I asked.

Half an hour later, I walked out of the store with a new brown saddle and two fly tying books. This time, I spent just over a hundred dollars.

What the books didn't say is that it isn't possible to learn fly tying from a book. If they had said that, they wouldn't have been published and I wouldn't have purchased them. After buying three more books, I had succeeded in tying another five Woolly Buggers. I returned to the shop to show Ray the results.

"*Not bad,*" Ray said, trying to not discourage me, "*This your design?*"

"*They're Woolly Buggers,*" I said.

"*Oh,*" Ray said.

He thoroughly examined the flies for several minutes.

Ray was very careful to conceal his amusement. "*You really should consider taking lessons,*" he said, "*we still have space in the beginner's class next week.*"

Jim Beaux taught the class. "*You bought a Regal?*" he asked, somewhat surprised. "*Most people start out with an inexpensive Indian-made vise.*"

"*Ray said I'd save money in the long run,*" I explained.

"*Oh,*" Jim said without smirking.

Six weeks later, I completed the beginner class. Jim encouraged me to take the next class so I could learn some advanced patterns. By the end of the fishing season, I had taken three more classes. I learned to tie using synthetic materials, how to work with deer and elk hair, how to make woven bodies, and everything else the professional tiers do.

A week later, I had tied several complicated patterns. The amortized cost of the flies was only thirty-five dollars seventy-two cents. Each. I decided to show Ray the results.

"*Not bad,*" he said, trying to not discourage me, "*Woolly Buggers?*"

"*Humpys.*"

"*Oh,*" Ray said.

The following spring, I returned to the Colorado Fly Fisher. I needed materials to tie flies for a trip to the Fryingpan. Ray sat at the vise, showing a customer how to tie a Royal Goofy Bug. When the customer was satisfied that he could duplicate the pattern, had purchased a hundred forty dollars' worth of materials and hooks to tie a half-dozen of them, he left.

I told Ray that he must tie many flies to fill his own box.

"*Hell no,*" Ray said, "*too much work. I just take 'em out of stock.*"

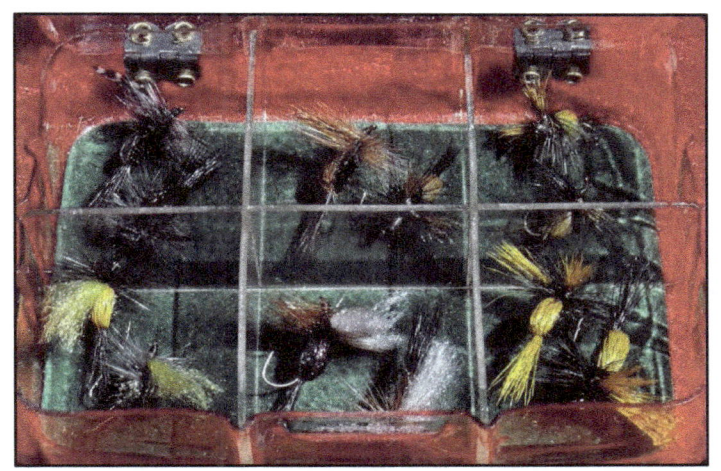

Al's fly box.

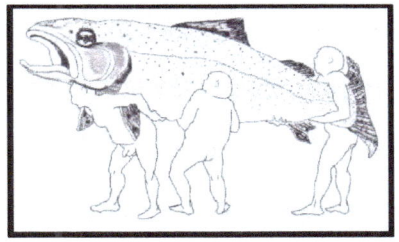

24. High-Tech Fly Fishing (by Al Marlowe)

"God Forbid You Drop Your Floatant!"

We are definitely living in the high-tech era. The revolution has even invaded the age-old sport of fishing. A visit to your favorite fly shop will leave you reeling after examining the new graphite rods, plastic fly lines, flies tied with synthetic materials, and neoprene waders. Vests are constructed of the latest acrylic fiber and reels are built of magnesium or titanium, making them extremely light. The only thing we haven't seen so far is a compound fly rod.

Anglers who have been in the sport more than a few years will recall the old-fashioned equipment. Fly rods were bamboo or fiberglass. Reels were made of heavy metals and flies were constructed of real feathers and fur. Because these natural materials were not water-repellant, they tended to absorb water quickly, causing them to sink rather than float high and dry. Though Mucilin was used, it didn't keep a fly dry for long.

Today, chemistry has given us a solution to this problem. On the shelves with the exotic rods and synthetic flies are high tech floatants. Whether in grease, liquid or spray form, these chemicals will make your fly waterproof down to 25 feet. Use of these floatants will absolutely prevent your fly from sinking – ever.

Each improvement, however, brings associated environmental problems. The EPA has really blown it on the floatants by not requiring an Environmental Impact Statement for use of such items.

My first experience with the new generation of floatants has prompted me to make fellow anglers aware of a potential problem. To avoid a possible lawsuit, the brand will not be mentioned. A few summers back, I fished a remote stream in the Colorado high country, which I will not identify for obvious reasons.

On this day, I had parked my truck near the river and fished upstream. In a few hours, I had covered nearly three miles of water. In the late afternoon a caddis hatch began. After treating an Elk Hair Caddis with one of the new floatants, I dropped the container before I could close it. The excitement of seeing 16-inch trout rising and the slipperiness of the plastic bottle combined to make me fumble it. Unable to locate the brightly colored container immediately and being eager to cast to the actively rising fish, I abandoned my brief search and started fishing.

I finished my angling endeavors that evening and returned to my truck. As I began to pack my gear, I noticed a pool in which a callibaetis hatch had begun and decided to make a few more last casts before quitting for the day.

As the light had started to fade and the fish were rising all around me, I failed to observe everything that happened on the water. While concentrating on changing flies in the near darkness, something bumped my leg. Being anxious to catch one more fish, I ignored it. Then it happened again. I felt another bump behind me. The fish were steadily rising, so again, I ignored it. After a minute or so, another object smashed into me, this time causing me to lose my balance and fall.

I was amazed at what I saw following my unplanned baptism. In the growing darkness, I observed rocks, from pebble size to boulders more than twenty inches in diameter (I did measure them) floating on the water. Not wishing to become a short item on the evening news I quickly stumbled my way out of the stream, dodging a growing number of rocks as I made my way to the bank.

The following day, I returned to the place where I had lost my floatant. What I saw was shocking. Not one rock was left on the stream bottom in this area. Apparently, the chemical had dissolved on contact with water and coated the rocks on the stream bottom, causing them to float.

A year later, I returned to this once lovely stretch of water, hoping to see that it had recovered from the previous year's disaster. What I found was disheartening. This former riffle was still a barren, mud-bottomed, fishless pool.

Perhaps it would be advisable for the manufacturers of these floatants to place warning labels on the containers. One company does state that an ounce of the chemical is sufficient to float the QE II all the way across the Atlantic to England. I would urge all fishermen using these products to recap them immediately after each use. Then, if the chemical should be inadvertently dropped in the water no harm will come to our streams and lakes.

There is one redeeming value for the new floatants. When the container is almost empty, tape the lid shut and pin it to your vest. The miniscule amount left inside the bottle makes it an excellent life preserver. Just don't get any of the stuff on the soles of your wading boots. You'll find yourself walking on water, scaring hell out of both fish and fishermen.

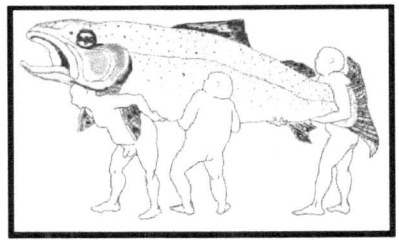

25. Stealth Fishing (by Al Marlowe)

"Belly up to the boat, boys"

There was a hint of astonishment in his voice. "You've never fished out of a float tube?" Ray Sapp, owner of The Colorado Angler in Lakewood, asked as we prepared for a three-day expedition to Taylor Park. When I replied, "No, I never have fished out of a float tube", he said he would bring one along for me to try. Little did I understand his motives.

Even if you haven't bought one yet, more than likely you've seen a lot of them floating the shallows and shorelines, resembling brightly colored donuts. You may have also noticed that anglers using them seem to do pretty well. Though not always the case, belly boaters are often into fishing when other anglers are just wishing. Are float tubes really that good?

Yes, they really are that good. And, no, fishing from one is no guarantee of catching fish. The reason for their effectiveness is that they are very sneaky. They're quiet. Anglers can get close to fish without spooking them. It's stealth fishing. A released fish may be as likely to hang around the protection of the tube as to swim away.

Perhaps in its extremely limited reasoning ability, the belly boat appears to be an over-sized lily pad.

Don't get the idea that belly boats are a new invention. 100-year old illustrations show similar, though primitive, floating platforms being used for fishing. While the refinements were few, they were likely just as effective as the latest models available today.

Fishing from a float tube for the first time is an interesting experience. My first question shouted to Ray was, "*How do I make it go?*" Actually, I was working too hard at it. After relaxing and settling down to kicking lightly, the tiny craft would go where ever I wanted with little effort. Turning is easy. Simply kick with one leg and drag the other.

Being a rather lazy way to fish, I settled on a single technique that first time out, one that I still favor - trolling. I tied an orange-and-brown Woolly Bugger to the leader and let the sinking line take it deep. By kicking easy and lightly twitching the rod tip, I could move backward at just the right speed to swim the leech imitation with an undulating motion over the bottom. With no more effort than that, I was able to take two fish on a slow, windy late-afternoon.

If by now, you're thinking you must have a float tube, there're a few things you'll want to consider. While a belly boat is a simple craft, the technology used in the design and construction isn't, at least in the good ones.

There's a lot more to 'em than a truck tire inner tube with a seat.

To begin with, buy the best one you can afford. An angler will want the assurance of a quality maker that the device isn't going to go flat far from shore in deep water. Fortunately, this doesn't have to mean spending a pile of dough. Just be wary of those of unknown origin featured in discount stores.

Look for a tube that allows you to sit upright in it. This will add greatly to comfort and maneuverability. You'll also want a boat with dual chambers, which current models have. The second chamber serves as a backrest, adding to comfort afloat. Lots of pockets are useful, too. You can store fly boxes, leaders, extra spools for your fly reel, and other little odds and ends. Some models feature a large pocket over the backrest. That's a good place to keep a rain jacket handy.

Once you have your float tube, there are a few other items you'll find helpful in enjoying the experience. Fishing most of Colorado's reservoirs and high lakes means low water temperatures. A belly boat angler rides low in the water rather than on it as in other boats. Neoprene chest-high waders are a necessity unless your fishing is for warm water species. You'll need to dress a little warmer for float tubing than you would when fishing from a boat or wading. Even with neoprene waders, the cold will be felt on all but the warmest days. A Gore-Tex® jacket will ward off the chills from mild breezes or brief rain-showers. A wool or polypropylene jacket, one that will keep you warm even when it gets damp, will keep you comfortable in 55-degree water.

Landing a fish from a float tube is challenging. The fish has the advantage. A net is a necessity, especially for the larger ones, which you will be catching now that you have a belly boat. A surgical clamp will be helpful for unhooking a fish. A mesh bag that hooks to the "O" rings on the boat serves to keep your catch fresh.

The easiest way to inflate a belly boat is with a small compressor that plugs into the lighter of your car. While the tube is being aired up, you can get into your waders and rig up your rod. If you plan to backpack your tube, a bicycle pump will do the job. A belly boat is properly inflated when the fabric is smooth all around, with no loose sags or bags.

Because a belly boat angler is so close to the water's surface, things like sunglasses and sunscreen are a necessity. On a bright day, you'll sunburn really easy. You might also want to use some artificial tears to reduce eye irritation caused by glare.

For personal comfort, an angler might want to consider drinking less coffee or other liquids before donning waders and paddling out a good distance from shore. If you need to be told why - well - you'll find out.

It is not possible to launch a float tube and look graceful doing it. First, get your fins on. Then unfasten the seat strap that goes between your legs. Place one foot inside the tube while trying not to fall down. Bring the other foot in and fasten the strap. Ideally, this is done while facing away from the water since you'll need to back in. Those large, floppy fins don't permit any other way.

Reach down and grab the nylon handles on each side and lift the tube up to your thighs. Now, walk backwards, preferably from a gentle incline, into the water. When the water gets up around your knees, sit down in the tube. Don't worry about looking silly launching the tube. Just smile. Every float tuber looks silly getting in the water.

Though spinning tackle can be used from a belly boat, fly fishing has more advantages. The fly angler has more choices of what to use, from tiny midge emergers to large Woolly Buggers and Zonkers. Because the fisherman sits so low, a long rod is advantageous for keeping the line off the water when casting. A good choice would be a nine or ten-foot graphite model throwing a 6-weight line. You'll want an extra spool or two so you can change from a floating to a sink-tip or full sinker as conditions dictate. When fishing deep, try a weighted fly or streamer on a sinking line and short leader. On or just below the surface, patterns like a Goddard Caddis or Rio Grande King in large sizes work well. Make a special effort to hit the damselfly hatch that occurs in late June and early July. Fishing it from a float tube lets you get out where the fish are without having to make long casts.

With all the lakes and reservoirs in Colorado, the float tube angler has plenty of places to fish. Many alpine lakes, being glacially carved, have shallow shelves around much of the shoreline. They are perfect for belly boating. The floating fisherman is able to get out past the shelf which anglers on the bank can't reach. A tube can be carried on a backpack or a pack animal. For short day trips, the inflated tube can be strapped to a pack frame with waders and fins stuffed into the middle. Pack it uninflated on a horse or llama to avoid problems, like spooking the animal or snagging it on low branches.

On large reservoirs, there is rarely a need to get out in deep water. Shallow weed beds, inlets and associated channels, and shorelines are made for float tubers. Fish will usually be concentrated in shallows near shore during feeding periods. Often, they will be cruising just out of range of anglers on the bank. Wading can get the fisherman a little closer to the fish, sometimes. Ski and bass-boats have limited ability to get into the shallows because of their draft. A canoe is a good choice of boat for shallow water but requires constant work with paddles to maintain position in a slight breeze or waves. A float tube, however, allows the angler to cast to feeding fish that are frequently out of range of the shoreline, in water too shallow for larger boats.

Remember that trout aren't the only fish you can take from a belly boat. Colorado's Front Range and Eastern plains have all kinds of warm water impoundments from irrigation reservoirs to small ponds stocked with bass and pan fish. Several South Park lakes in Central Colorado hold northern pike and will readily take a large fly.

Now that float tubes are selling faster than donuts at a coffee shop, the makers are coming out with new features and innovations. There's one for backpackers that needs no inner tube, reducing weight. There are rectangular boats and one with a V shaped stern. A new, radical design on another type features a U shape, making it easy to launch since the angler doesn't have to crawl inside the tube. There's even one made of solid foam. While it can't be punctured, neither can it be deflated to carry in a compact car. Actually, it's hard to improve on the basic design but if the makers didn't produce new models, you wouldn't buy them, would you?

While float tubes are a pleasure to use, there are a few safety considerations to observe. You'll want to buy the best float tube you can afford. Your life depends on it. Stay out of the middle of a lake. If a storm approaches, you don't want to be caught too far from shore. Most often, the fish are in the shallows, anyway.

Use common sense. Don't try anything that is obviously hazardous. While it shouldn't need to be said, don't get out of your belly boat in middle of lake. Because the angler sits low in the water, the tube is very stable and able to handle rough water. And since your fins provide your only power, use good ones. Your dealer can help you select the most suitable fins.

A view of Spinney Reservoir as seen from a belly boat.

Don't belly boat alone and avoid going on the water at ice-out. A tuber can become trapped between ice flows.

Make yourself visible to boaters. Some belly boats have a large, fluorescent orange patch that can be seen easily. Be extra cautious around boaters if you're using a camo model.

For as much fun and as effective as they are, there are places you can't take your new float tube. Most city ponds and reservoirs have regulations prohibiting their use. In other legal aspects, you won't have to register it, at least not in Colorado. On at least two lakes, the use of a Coast Guard approved flotation device is required; Bear Creek Reservoir in Lakewood and Georgetown Reservoir along I-70. You may want to use an emergency flotation device anyway in the unlikely event that both chambers should go flat.

Float tube fishing is sneaky. It's stealth fishing. And it's simple. You won't have to learn any nautical language; no bowlines, no port or starboard. You won't need to scuttle the portholes or batten down the mizzenmast. All you need to do is have fun catching fish.

By the way, Ray and I returned from our expedition on a Tuesday. On Thursday afternoon, I bought a float tube from him. Three hours later, I had taken five rainbows while fishing from it. With all due respect to The Western Company's TV commercials of a few years back: If you don't have a belly boat, get one.

Belly-boater with a Rainbow on Spinney Reservoir, in South Park, Colorado (life vest is under the blouse in this photo.)

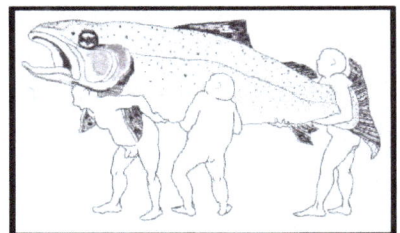

26. The Fishing Pole Thief (by Al Marlowe)

One fella's trash is another man's pole."

The 16-inch rainbow had taken my fly with abandon and run downstream. Because I was concentrating on the fish and worrying about the 7-X tippet, I hadn't noticed the scruffy looking young man until I finally led the heavy-bodied fish to the bank to unhook it. I said hello or some such greeting. He didn't reply.

Instead, he took a step closer to me and put his hands in the pockets of the dirty and tattered camo jacket he wore. Indicating that he may have a weapon in his pocket, he finally spoke. "*Gimme your fish pole,*" he said, sort of grunting.

"*What?*" I asked.

"*Gimme your fish pole,*" he said again. I hesitated. He stepped closer, reaching out with his left hand while keeping his right in the pocket, making it appear to contain a gun.

"*You gotta be kidding,*" I said. "*You want this stuff? Why?*"

Instead of being agitated, he began to offer an explanation of why he wanted my fishing tackle. "*There's too much risk and too little return from knocking off a gas station or quick stop,*" he said. "*I've noticed all the yuppies who've taken up fly fishing. I know their poles cost lots of money. I can get a lot more from selling your pole than I could by holding up some joint. Now gimme your stuff.*"

"*Well,*" I said trying to stall while thinking of a plan to keep from getting ripped off, "*You're certainly right about the yuppies. In fact, they've ruined the sport of fly fishing. But you'd do much better by finding a real yuppie to rob.*"

"*Huh?*" he said, "*Whadda ya mean?*"

I had judged this would-be fish pole thief correctly. He knew nothing about fishing tackle except that yuppies bought expensive stuff. I motioned for him to come closer.

"*You really want this rod?*" I asked incredulously. "*Look closer.*"

I showed him my handmade rod I had built on a Sage blank.

"*Looks alright tuh me,*" he said, "*Now gimme it.*"

"*Not so fast,*" I said. "*First, you need to see what you're getting. See these wraps,*" I said, letting him examine the rod. "*I couldn't afford to buy a factory made rod like the *yuppie anglers. So, I built this one. No, I didn't build the graphite blank. But what I did was buy a kit. I don't have a lot of money like the yuppies do so it was a way to save a few bucks. Trouble is, I screwed up on this one. Look at how bad those wraps are. And the guide spacing's all wrong."*

He grunted as though he knew what I was showing him.

"Now, read the name on the rod," I said.

"Sage?" he said, *"So what?"*

"So what?" I said, *"So it shows you have a lot to learn. This isn't a Sage, it's an Osage. You couldn't tell because the decal is worn. Osage is one of the cheapest rods you can buy. Definitely not worth stealing. In fact, if you want it, take it. You'll be doing me a favor."*

"Huh," he said in surprise, *"I don't understand."*

"If you plan to get rich stealing fish poles," I said, *"you better start reading Fly Rod Angler. Then you'd know that Osage is a cheap foreign made copy of the Sage rod. Wish I could afford one. That's what all those yuppies are buying."*

"But you seemed to throw that string pretty good with it. If it's junk, how come it works OK for you?"

"If you still think it's so good," I said, *"Here. You try it."* I handed him the rod. On his first cast, he snagged the brush behind us. After I unhooked it, he tried again and piled the line in front of his feet.

"*I see what you mean,*" he said. "*But how come you throw it so good?*"

"*I've been using it for nearly six years,*" I explained, "*When you use something that long, you learn to adjust even if it is inferior.*"

"*What about that winch?*" he asked, "*It looks pretty good to me.*"

At first I wasn't sure what he meant. Then I figured out he was talking about my Hardy Marquis reel.

"*Oh, you mean this reel,*" I said with disgust. "*Take it, too, if you want it. I'll file a claim with my insurance company and tell them I had some good stuff. Then maybe I could afford to get something decent.*"

"*But it don't look junky,*" he said.

"*Look at the name,*" I said sarcastically.

"*Hardy,*" he said as if proud of his reading skills.

"*Now look at where it was made,*" I said.

He squinted, then said, "*Made in England.*"

"*Right,*" I said.

"*I don't get it,*" he said.

"*If you're going to survive as a fish pole thief,*" I said, "*I can see you need someone to teach you the finer points of the sport. Everyone knows that the finest reel made is the Hardly. And it's made in the good ole US of A. This*

Hardy is a cheap imitation. Bought it at K-Mart. It's made for people like me who can hardly afford a Hardly."

I chuckled disgustedly at my own joke. The scruffy looking man chuckled too, as if he was beginning to understand.

"While we're on the subject of reels, not winches as you called them," I said, *"you might as well learn about some of the other names you'll encounter among yuppie anglers. One to definitely avoid is a Hoss. They're cheap copies of Ross reels. The Hoss, like my pole, is made in Asia and sells for just a couple of bucks. Steal one and you might as well throw it in the nearest dumpster. But if you should find a genuine Ross, well that's something else."*

"Oh," I said as an afterthought, *"another name to avoid is the Gabel. They give those Gabels away in boxes of Cracker Jacks."*

He gave me a puzzled look.

I went on to explain that he should try to find the one named Disabel. *"They're called that because any fish caught with it is going to be permanently disabled."*

"Yeah," he said grinning, *"I get it."*

The smirk left his face and he began to look despondent. *"I was thinking about taking your rubber overalls but I suppose they're cheap, too,"* he said.

"*You got it,*" I said. "*These Rott waders leak like a sieve. In fact, I wonder why I bother wearing them. Underneath, my pants are soaking wet. I might as well be wading without 'em.*"

I paused to let my words soak in. He looked at me kind of puzzled.

"*Sure wish I could afford some of those Scott waders,*" I said with a faraway look.

"*Scott?*" he asked.

"*Scott,*" I said.

"*But I thought Scott was whiskey,*" he said.

"*You got it,*" I replied. "*In fact, I could stand a drink right now. It's sorta like the name of the finest waders available. But, man, they're sure expensive. Just like a fine 12-year old single-malt Scotch whiskey.*"

He looked at me as if questioning what I had just told him.

"*Look,*" I said as I pulled my waders down to my knees and showed him my sweat-dampened jeans. "*If I was wearing Scott waders, I'd be dry as a bone.*"

"*But why do you wear these if they don't keep you dry,*" the young man asked.

"*It's all I can afford,*" I replied meekly. "*If I had money like those yuppies, I'd have some good waders, too.*" I made the word "*yuppie*" sound almost vulgar.

He was silent for a moment. Then he noticed my vest and five boxes of flies. He pointed to one box and demanded to see it. I opened the box and handed it to him.

"Gimme all your boxes of these feather bugs," he said. *"They gotta be worth something."*

"They're called flies," I said, showing a little contempt as I gained confidence that I was winning the battle of wits. After all, he was unarmed, defenseless. Well, maybe he was half armed. *"And I made them myself, just like I made my pole, I mean rod."*

"You made these?" he asked in surprise.

"Right," I said. *"Couldn't afford to pay two dollars for one of those feather bugs at a fly shop. So, I make 'em myself. They work. Of course, they're not as good as the ones you buy."*

The young man was handing me my fly box as Glen Smedley, the local game warden stepped out of the willows along the bank.

"How's fishing, Al?" he asked, *"Doing any good? Who's your buddy?"*

"Caught and released a 16-incher a few minutes ago," I said. *"And this man isn't a friend. In fact, he just tried to rob me."*

The young man started to run but was halted by Glen's strong hand gripping his arm. Glen soon had him cuffed and his rights read.

"You know, I think this feller's the one who just held up the Yummie Freeze in town. Got away with $17.54. He take your money?"

"Nope," I said, "*He just tried to take my fish pole.*"

"*Well,*" Glen said, *"It looks like his thieving days are over. Now go back to your fishing. There's a two-footer in that hole around the bend. Saw 'im just yesterday. Oh. I'll probly have to subpoena you for this case. Don't catch more'n your limit, Al.*"

Glen left with his prisoner, I began shaking. I struggled to fasten my waders and walked down to the bend pool on rubbery legs to try for the fish he told me about. My casting wasn't much better than that of the man who tried to take my Sage. In spite of the splash I made with the #18 BWO, the fish took. I forgot about the 7X leader and set the hook too hard. The fish was gone, taking my hand-tied fly with him. I had enough for one day and waded ashore nearly falling in when I bumped against a submerged log and headed back to the truck. My tackle was put away and I was about to open the door when I saw a scruffy looking man wearing a dirty camo jacket heading my way. "*Any luck?*" he asked when he got closer. "Yeah," I told my brother, "*all bad. Now get in and let's go.*"

27. Fly fishing the Futa - A Trip to Chile (by Karen Rae Christopherson)

"By all means – tease it and keep stripping!"

It was January 16th - I got a call from a client (my real job is that of a geophysicist) saying, "Can you go to Chile on the 25th?" My rapid response was, "YES!" because the back of my mind was thinking not of work, but of the supreme opportunity for fly fishing.

Step One - Call the travel agent and book a fare to Santiago. I needed four days there for the job.

Step Two - Contact several fly fishing outfitters in southern Chile on short notice. One outfitter, whom I had met just weeks earlier at the Denver Fly Fishing Show, had no clients booked for the EXACT four days I would be there. YAHOO! - my fishing dreams are about to come true.

It's quite an exciting journey to go fly fishing in Chile. Getting to Santiago is just the first step, requiring about 20 hours of traveling time from Denver via Miami. Then, the trip entails flying from Santiago to Puerto Montt (about 600 miles south and 1.5 hours by air). Then, another puddle jumper flight to Chaiten (an additional 100 miles south and 45 minutes flying). Finally, take a 2.5-hour van ride east, close to the Argentine border, and home to one of the largest, most beautiful rivers I have ever seen in my life, the Futaleufú.

Karen on the Futa.

The Futaleufú starts in Patagonia and bends westward across the Andes through Chile to Lago Yelcho for 153 miles. Chile is comprised of glacial valleys and fjords, reminiscent of coastal Alaska but with better weather. The mountain walls are steep and topped with glaciers and snowfields. The Futa is aqua blue, and incredibly clear. In January, it is summer there- equivalent to July in North America.

The origin of the Futaleufú flowing from Argentina into Chile.

Fly fishing in this region is a relatively new tourist venue because the road was constructed only 20 years ago. Most of the visitors are kayakers and rafters who flock to the Futa for its series of class V+ waters. However, several long stretches of the river are flat water and home to

Brown and Rainbow trout. Both of these trout species were introduced on the Argentine side of the river almost 100 years ago. The Brown trout originate from Europe; the Rainbows from McCloud River stock out of California. Over the years they have flourished and grown to become wild fish that do not know what an artificial fly is - chances are that a fish you hook will have never tasted a wooly bugger or Chernobyl ant before.

The two guides: Joe and Joshua -Joe caught this big Brown while wading on the edge of a gravel bar. He was very excited. It's nice to see an experienced guide get excited.

This is a BIG river - 10,000 to 12,000 CFS - hard to find that in Colorado or Wyoming. The best method is by floating in a dory. My guides (Joe and Joshua) were actually from Durango, Colorado spending their winter by working in Chile. Fishing with an outfitter in Chile normally means that they supply everything - your housing, food, transportation.

Floating on the Futa was like a dream. The Caribbean Sea-looking water reminded me of bone fishing in the ocean flats, not trout fishing. Some of the pools were still and at least 20 feet deep. Peering over the raft edge you could see trout suspended in the water. A quiet cast and a stripped streamer on the surface would draw them in a chase to the surface. It's a wonderful thing to watch trout chase flies, especially from a long distance.

Rafts landed on the beach.

Big river and wild trout country means big rods - a 6 or 7 wt with strong leader and tippet. These fish are fighters -

many people remark that hooking a 14-inch Rainbow on the Futa seems to put up the fight of a 22-inch Rainbow at home. The flies of choice for this venue would be large as well - wooly buggers, Madame X's, Bitch Creeks, large stimulators mostly plopped, moved, and stripped to get the trout interested in chasing what they perceive as a good meal. After much complaining from me about the heavy flies, my guide allowed me to use a huge Chernobyl ant - luckily the fish were interested in dries that day.

When one of the wild browns on the Futa becomes interested in your fly, you can see him line up. You have to tease him – "*STRIP! STRIP! STRIP!*" (the guide yelled at me) There is no margin for messing around and waiting for the trout to just grab the thing. The trout will chase around the water looking like a cross between a submarine and an alligator. "TEASE IT! KEEP STRIPPING!" yelled the guide. Finally, the guide yelled "SET!!!" and thank heaven (with dread) I have to land this huge walrus. Whew! Who knew fly fishing could be so much work. Ahh, but the reward – what a magnificent fish. Released, now, fish = free; me = happy. And then I am ready to do it all over again!

Karen with a big grin and a big brown on the Futa.

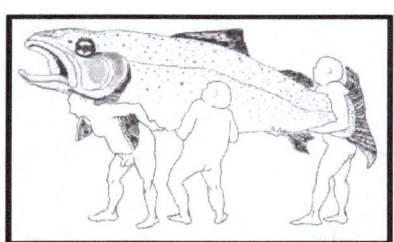

28. Whitewater Fly fishing (by Karen Rae Christopherson)

"White water fishing whether you want o or not."

When I was about 40 I married a Canadian. We had a lot of important priorities in common – basically any outdoor activity. He moved down to the USA with his large red truck, some clothes, and his indispensable water distiller – no guns, no toys, just the basics.

A couple of years later we were living in a rural type of community within a Denver suburb (yes, those do exist) getting something fixed by a farmer (living on a parcel of farm land) when my husband spied a canoe lying in the grass of the neighbors' yard. His Canadian blood boiled.

"*I have to have that.*" He said. So, we went to the neighbor and bought it for $150.

I didn't know what it was, specifically, that called to my husband's heart about his canoe. I imagined us paddling around a lake with the ducks. Romantic. But no, this was a specialized 17 foot Grumman aluminum whitewater canoe. '*What?*' I thought. I had kayaked and rafted down some pretty serious rivers in Colorado, but white water canoeing? Canoes were for lakes, like in Wisconsin. Right?

My Canadian husband knew differently. They (Canadians) take the whole whitewater canoe thing pretty seriously. He started talking to me about keels and flotation. After all, he had once been an instructor teaching the Canadian army how to paddle a whitewater canoe. (Don't ask why. It's a Canadian thing.)

So, I had to start learning about paddling the dumb thing and listening to his commands, um, "cues". We started out on a lake for a few times, then we began paddling down the Blue River outside of Silverthorne, Colorado many more times (pretty easy to do if you watch out for low bridges).

This level of paddling was ok to manage even though once in a while we navigated some class II water with riffles. All seemed to be going well in consideration that I was settling down to float less challenging runs than class V rapids in my kayaking days of old.

One morning, after a 2-hour paddle trip down the Blue River north of Frisco, he wanted to try more challenging water and I said (like an idiot). "*Well, the Colorado River is only about a half hour drive from here*".

"*Let's go!*" he said.

We arrived at Pumphouse in early afternoon. There was no one else around. A sign sticking out of the bank warned: "*Caution high water – proceed with caution.*" (It was running about 12,000 CFS that day.) I looked at my husband with trepidation. (See Figure 44 – in *Salmon flies in the Colorado*....)

"*We'll be fine.*" he assured me. There was one other craft launching. It was a raft with four people and two coolers (a good sign of quasi-serious rafters, i.e., party boat).

"*Hey, will you watch our backs in case we get in trouble?*" asked the husband.

"*Sure!*" they said happily giggling.

Off we went. We had wetsuits, life jackets, flotation (well, a sort of kind of flotation – we tied inflated inner-tubes to the cross-members of the canoe). My husband sat in back (as always, yelling, um, providing directions to me).

After a bit of successful navigations of mere eddies and low rockers of knee high waves, we turned a corner, (he was swatting at mosquitos), and the nose of the canoe got sucked into the hydraulic of an upcoming HUGE TONGUE – a drop in the river that leads into a huge standing wave. (Later we realized that this structural passage was called Eye of the Needle Rapid where a lady had died only one week earlier). Jim stopped swatting at flies mid-air and opened his mouth to start yelling (directing) a command to save our lives – too late. We got sucked into the hole.

Eye of the Needle is a channel of swift water pouring over boulders and dropping into frothy tongues of white water that can be relatively easy to navigate as long as the oarsmen avoid one immanent feature: the "Eye of the Needle", which is a one-way tunnel scoured into the vertical wall of granite about canoe level on the left. The hydraulics of the system flush the main body of water into the tunnel, which chokes down into a tiny tube and acts like a sieve to trap debris in the tunnel with no way out.

All I remember from this particular incident was looking up at the top of the water from inside my life vest. I really did see my life flash before my eyes. Time seemed to lag forever as I was washed to sea. I was also aware (and mad) that I had lost my expensive sunglasses. My world was made up of water swirling. Nothing else. Water.

Then, I was being physically dragged by the collar of my vest to shore by the husband. Boat = gone. Large rocks = numerous. But I still had my paddle! (My husband had told me "never let go of your paddle.")

I was mad (and wet and cold and frightened but mostly mad). I started walking up the rocks in my wetsuit booties. The railroad tracks were just above. I knew we were going to have to walk a couple of miles to get to the next station of human access, downstream at Radium. This is remote country.

I had to pee – badly. So, I committed myself to the laborious task of pulling down my tight fitting wetsuit and then squatted on the railroad tracks. At that exact moment when the bladder releases and the hot stream is flowing without retribution and without recall, whistle and then the engine of the Amtrak California Zephyr passenger train came charging around the bend. I managed to waddle my bond ankles to the very tippy edge of the tracks enough to avoid being run over as the tourists in the dome car gapped at the wildlife: some strange tall thin naked gal with a paddle at her feet peeing next to the tracks trying to look as if she might possibly be invisible, which she was not.

With that embarrassing moment behind me (no pun intended) we moved on – still mad – I walked ahead of my husband with my paddle in my hand. Then, I saw a coal train from OTHER direction, slowly coming head-on from around another bend. He was going really slowly. Oddly slow. I hunkered over to the side of the track. The train kept slowing down. Then, of course, it stopped next to me. The engineer leaned out the window and yelled,

"Hey, did you lose a silver canoe?" (And are you the lady who was peeing on our tracks? I thought to myself.)

I said, *"Yes – we did!"* with glorious ownership of the situation, like maybe the paddle was a clue, and he answered that it was wrapped around a rock downstream. Great! It's waiting for us to get back in and try this all over again. There are only 14 more miles and a few more class IV rapids to get through along the way…. No problem.

We finally hiked close enough to Radium that we could cross the river on a bridge. There was a guy sitting in an SUV who obviously had too many beers but offered to drive us back to our car. We accepted.

The canoe was found by a bunch of rafties that hang out in Radium. They had somehow managed to retrieve the raft off the rock. I went to pick it up – gave them $100 – we pounded out the dents later.

That big ol' canoe now sits in the grass in our yard. A lawn ornament.

A couple of years later, my husband was trying to figure out how to get back to the white water thing. He knew I loved fly fishing. He had gotten jealous when male friends took me float fishing on a raft. So, when we went to the Denver Fly fishing Show and he saw a pontoon drift boat – I could see the light bulbs flashing in his mind.

Of course, we bought the boat.

Wow! Now I had my personal oarsman! He would rather row than fish, so I had it made. He built a special platform for the dog, too. He made every little thing organized. Off we went to fly-fish the rivers of Colorado.

I had a new rule now, though, about rivers and float fishing: Nothing bigger than Class II. Fat chance. He didn't know how to estimate the grade of river rapids. After a few times of too much water in my face and trying to rescue my very expensive fly rod, I got serious about what water I would float. When there was rough water – I got out and walked downstream while he and the dog had "fun".

It all eventually worked out in the end. We've taken the boat-bone-fishing in the Bahamas, lake fishing, and yes, whitewater fishing. We no longer have this particular dog, but now the husband is trying to fit a cage on the deck so our cat can travel with us.

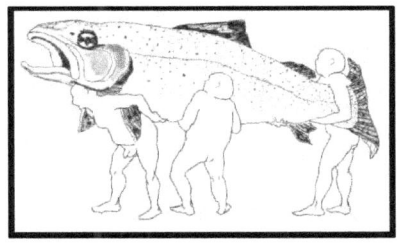

29. I Wanted a Fishing Dog (by Karen Rae Christopherson)

"We became a trio, a team of 3 outdoor spirits."

I wanted a fishing dog, or maybe a hunting dog. Specifically, I wanted a black Lab. I had two older dogs, past their years of hiking and fishing who were now enjoying retirement as "squirrel watchers." A younger dog had been on my 'wish list' for a while.

My husband, Jim, wanted a Standard Poodle. Luckily for me, Standards were hard to come by at that time. Jim was working in Winter Park, Colorado and he read in the Thrifty Nickel paper one day, *"For Sale – black Lab puppies"*. Off we went to Hot Sulphur Springs.

The dog family lived in an odd looking dilapidated A-frame cabin with the mom Lab, the puppies, and also a mixture of kittens and young human children. All these babies were playing together. There was one particular puppy that seemed especially friendly. I knew that one would be a good dog from living and playing with all that love and joy bouncing around in that home. The family had named him Raider – not for a football team - but for the Raiders of the Lost Ark movie series. That was a fine name for this dog. He came pre-packaged with good Fishing-Dog Karma.

I was tasked with puppy care almost every day because the husband worked from 6 a.m. to 4 p.m... I played with Raider, taught him things, and soon took him with me fishing.

It was winter, so I would tie him to a tree while I fished an ice-free section of the South Platte River. After a while, we'd move upstream and I would tie Raider to tree then fish some more. Raider was very content just watching.

As Raider got bigger, he became more interested in the ice, the stream, and in particular the fish. I took to tying him to my wading belt. This initiated two lessons for us both... 1) Raider fell through the ice edge on the river and learned that he could swim, which meant I would never keep him out of the stream again; and 2) I learned that if another large dog showed up nearby, Raider would bound at it and pull me down onto my knees on the rocks. Needless to say, this changed the way in which we fished together.

Our fishing journeys continued through the spring and the summer. By then, Jim had negotiated a career change (quit his job), and opted for a job that gave him more time at home and options for mini-vacations.

My husband doesn't really like fly fishing. Buying him a really nice Hardy Rod and Reel just wasn't enough enticement to set the hook. So, husband began to dog-tend while I fished. Soon, Jim got the idea to tie a bobber on the fly line, cast, and Raider would chase it downstream. Oh, what fun! Dog Fun! - Especially when they decided to do this while standing near me. To hell with the fish! The dog wants to play! Fetch!

My fishing dog soon became Jim's fun dog. They went on walks together. They went on drives in the truck together. He taught Raider how to be on a leash while he rode his mountain bike (a few incidents occurred when the dog chased a deer or rabbit on the other side of the bike).

Jim needed a way to exercise the dog for longer runs. Eventually, he discovered that when he rode his Trials motorcycle Raider would happily run alongside. Together, they ventured into canyon lands, saw petroglyphs, swam in high country lakes. Sadly, I had come to realize I had lost my fishing dog partner probably for good.

Raven overlooking the Colorado River above Radium.

However, Jim soon had the bright idea we should get a cata-raft so we could float down rivers while I fish. I imagined my own personal guide on the river and floating down nice quiet stretches of the Arkansas or Gunnison. Ha! – that is apparently not what my Canadian, ex-whitewater canoeist husband had in mind! So, we settled for stretches of river with a combination of rapids and flat water. Then, I actually did have my own personal guide/oarsman with some excitement thrown in.

But Raider? It looked like the dog would have to stay behind now. So, the husband cleverly devised and built a special platform for Raider. The dog loved it. We would stop, let the dog swim, get him back in and continue downriver. This worked fairly well, except when there was a deer on shore and a sudden dog-leap tilted the boat wildly, the dog bounding away as we both yelled and grabbed for balance (I had to protect my damn expensive fly-rod too!)

It was also quite a challenge to land a fish – two people, one dog, fish-on, in a rapid current. The fish was excited, the dog was jumping around, the boat was twirling, the line and fish would go under the boat. But at the least, we had a fishing dog and eh was always with us having a great time.

Nature and Time have their duty. Age plays her hand. As Raider got older he couldn't run as far, though his heart wanted to. Jim knew the dog would have to ride part of the way on our motorbike journeys (by this time my husband had convinced me to get a dirt bike on my own with the temptation of, "*Think how much faster you can get to those high mountain lakes!*". This clever ploy worked). Jim also bought a new motorcycle, sort of. He found a Rokon aka Tote-Goat – a 2WD motorcycle that sounds like a lawnmower and can go up anything, riding on ATV tires.

He taught the dog, with much patience, to ride on a platform that he built on the rear of the Rokon. He trained Raider to commands about when to get off and on and to sit quietly. The big old dog loved it and would ride with this head on Jim's shoulder.

Raven learning his new perch.

Raven really enjoying himself.

We did this for many years – travelling around the backcountry of Colorado, Utah and Wyoming – up hills, thru desert, down to rivers. We shared our time and our lunches with Raider. We always had a plan to find a pond, stock tank, or a creek so Raider would have water to drink and play. We became a trio, a team of 3 outdoor spirits, (one of whom loved fishing.)

Raider didn't have his usual spunk one summer. We thought it might be worms. It was worse, though – cancer. He died in Jim's arms in the back of our Jeep on the way to the vet's. We haven't adopted another dog but we now have a cat that goes camping and accompanies us on walks. Jim is devising ways to take the cat on the boat.

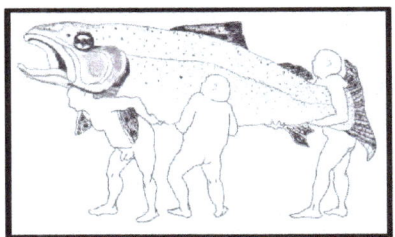

Karen finally enjoying her fishing dog.

30. Elmo the Fishing Snob (by Michele White "Murray")

"Never underestimate the ability of a dog to become a snob about something he knows he has mastered."

I took my three dogs in the car with my rods and headed toward one of two destinations: either the river or the hot springs. By the time I got halfway across South Park I saw that the Middle Fork of the South Platte was just starting to drop down from flooding. The water was running big and clear through the Hartsel Springs Ranch pasture - the north end of which is public access. I could see a car was already parked there and I did have three dogs after all so I couldn't fish at that access.

'Bummer,' I said to myself.

I was driving on a dirt road following the river downstream through South Park, Colorado along the Middle Fork of the South Platte River to its confluence with the South Fork of the South Platte where the Hartsel Springs Dude Ranch is actually located – (a private establishment marked with no trespassing signs). I drove onto the ranch property anyway and drove past cabins looking into windows of the lodge to see if anyone was there but the place was vacant. I returned to my car and was on my way out when a crappy little clown car full of rough looking stinky cowboys (old ones) drove up with a not so friendly look on their faces and I said to them:

"Hi there - do you guys work here? I used to know Dick and Wendy Grummet who used to own the ranch and they used to let me fish here - would you consider letting me fish here?", which was mostly true, in that I did know Dick and Wendy, but that fact is a bit of a touchy statement because the Grummets were not loved by everyone in the region depending on who you talked to. You never know if you were talking to a friend or enemy of them plus I was not that partial to them myself. I never did take advantage of fishing on their ranch because of that.

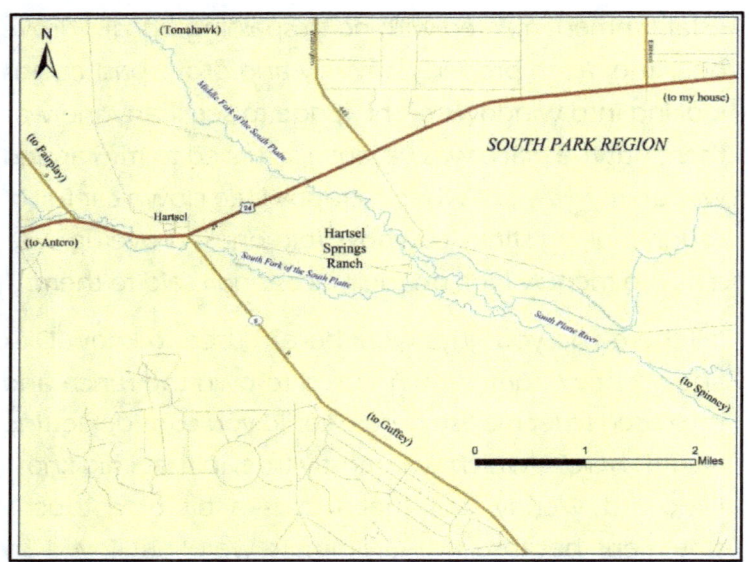

The confluence of the Middle Fork and the South Fork of the South Platte River.

The cowboys were not so willing to let me fish the river that flows through their pasture and they mentioned the many other public access spots to me. So, I countered with the fact that I have three dogs and the public access spots were already taken by other anglers. I only wanted to fish for a little while from about their bridge to maybe 500 feet upstream. They looked me over and eventually said OK because they weren't such bad guys after all.

I backed my car up to their pasture gate, changed into my rubber pants, sprayed myself and the black dog heads with fly spray and climbed the gate. Dogs scooted under the barbed wire fence.

The South Platte River in this vicinity has Brown trout uniformly about 8-12 inches long and a few rare ones maybe 17-18 inches – but rarely do you catch the larger ones. I have fished this river rather regularly for about 12 or so years. Brown Brown Brown Brown trouties about 8-12 inches is what this river gives ya. That is the South Platte River story in the vicinity below Hartsel. Above Hartsel you get into Brookies as well because the Middle Fork of the South Platte runs directly off the Continental Divide at Hoosier Pass, (Boreas Pass run-off goes into Tarryall River). The smaller chilly water of the Middle Fork north of highway 24 and upstream of the Hartsel Springs Ranch in the Tomahawk basin is dammed by beavers into ponds linked together by little creeks. The beaver work makes a perfect habitat for both Browns and Brookies. This day, however, I wanted to fish on the ranch in order to catch larger trout.

So, I was mystified that on my first cast above the bridge at the ranch I caught a small 7 or 8-inch rainbow. I had to examine it to prove to myself it was what I thought it was: '*This is a rainbow trout.*' Then, I caught another and another.

Here is the fish story part of this tale:

Elmo LOVES to see and catch a fish. He watches the river at the riffles and eddies because he has learned if he holds still he might see a trout snout. He stalks them. Elmo will gently enter the water without making a splash and sneak up on a trout then snag it in the shallow water. He has done this enough times that I know it is not a fluke. Elmo is a fishing dog. (The part of this story I am reluctant to share because most people roll their eyes is that Elmo will watch me cast as well - he watches the dry fly floating on a drift to see if he can watch for the moment the trout takes the fly. He will sit on the bank and watch my fly like a vulture and then stand with tail wagging when a fish takes the fly.)

Elmo looking for a rise.

Needless to say, when I do get a fish on it is really hard to keep Elmo off the fish. He will absolutely defy me and at the least come stand nose to nose with the trout exercising all his control as I yell and demand of him NO NO NO ELMO NO!!!! because I know that sometimes

Elmo's instinct to bite the trout is too overwhelming too irresistible - he will bite the trout, which is totally unfair to the slippery, finned animal.

Elmo fishing by himself on the North Platte.

Yesterday, in the Hartsel Springs Ranch north pasture on the Middle Fork of the South Platte River above its confluence with the South Fork, about 500 feet above the bridge, I caught a 20+ inch rainbow trout (on a hopper against the bank). I felt the weight of this fish before I saw it breach the surface. I was fishing from inside a hiding place of wild rose bushes (yellow ones) from an overhang of the bank and the river was super deep and running strong there. Elmo was way across the pasture with my other Labrador, Sage, hunting rabbits.

Maddie (the quiet good dog) is always right behind me, a non-entity for fishing.

Typical stance: Maddie one step behind and Elmo looking for a trout.

I did not have a net.

This large trout could not be landed by hand at this place because I was going to need to be in the water to straddle it in order to wrench the hopper from its snout with a hemostat (pliers). I led the trout downstream along the bank with my rod doubled in half wondering if the line would hold, would the rod break, would the trout run for cover - which it did - the line went ZZZZZzzzzzzzz off my reel and the trout took off for the far side of the stream. It swam downstream and went under a branch of a submerged log. I wrangled the line and rod and trout within the margins of a miracle to free the snag without breaking the line. This bank-side expenditure of energy is what attracted Elmo like a shark. He saw my antics from afar and he knew I had a trout on - a BIG ONE.

Just as I relieved the trout of its snag on the log, I saw a black sea monster churning upstream toward me from the quieter water of the main current. Its shoulders dipped from side to side with powerful strokes. Its eyes were bulging at my big trout. Even the trout saw this dog coming and it froze. It was my personal obligation to not only to free this poor trout from the hook but also to save it from the jaws of Elmo before he was upon us.

I used the rod and line to drag the trout past Elmo downstream and I let the huge trout dive under Elmo like a submarine all the while yelling - NO NO NO ELMO NO!!!! STOP IT BAD DOG!!!!!! Elmo turned in the stream like a barge as if he had sonar built in to pick up the submerged body of the trout. I let my line direct the trout downstream and Elmo followed. (He knows how to read a line in the water!) I used my most authoritative mean angry voice NO ELMO! B-A-D DOG!! NO! but Elmo was listening to an inner voice, one from Jack London. The Call of the Wild was upon him: *Get that Trout!* it said.

The trout dove into the mainstream of the powerful current and I ran alongside as Elmo followed the trout into the stronger water. Elmo's body began to be swept downstream by the tide and I was relieved to see that there was a place in the bank I could step down and stand on a rock to let this fish go. As I made my way carefully down to the swollen water (not wearing a life vest mind you and I am prone to falling in), I saw out of the corner of my eye, the black sea monster returning UPSTREAM against the full current with his shoulders making each stride count against the flow - ELMO was making headway swimming upstream to GET THAT GREAT TROUT!!

I nearly had the trout at my side. Elmo approached. I jabbed my fingers through the handles on the hemostats and pointed the grabbers toward the trout face. I could see that it was a giant rainbow. The trout flinched. Elmo was nearly upon us. I grabbed at the haft of the hopper and missed. Elmo snapped his jaws at my trout but I let it dive again. NO NO NO ELMO BAD DOG. The trout was in a state of shock by now, held captive by its upper jaw, the hopper stuck tight into the roof of its mouth. I made a final grab at the fly, got the haft of the hook and released the trout as Elmo surged on top of us.

We both watched the huge, fat silvery beast sink beneath Elmo's torso into the deep part of the stream. We let that big rainbow go back to where trouts belong. Elmo would not get out of the water. I hooked a couple more rainbows after I had recovered from the big one and each time came Elmo paddling up to me like a manatee bulging big eyes at the splashing fish. I let him watch. The trouts let go of my flies and we all eventually came home with one helluva trout story day. Even Elmo.

Elmo wearing his rain suit.

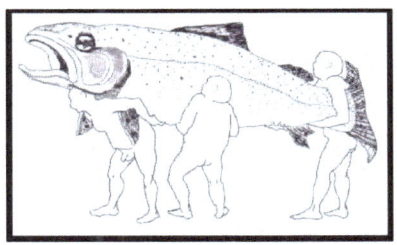

31. Mid-October on the Gunnison River (by Michele White "Murray")

"There is nothing like a 10-day fishing vacation lying in front of you to inspire the fickle finger of fate to take a poke."

We like to fish the Gunnison River above Delta, Colorado because in mid-October, the temperature there is still warm enough to enjoy camping out and wearing shorts and sandals one more time before winter sets in. We take a ten-day trip in mid-October to cast and blast, enjoying grouse, Chukar, duck and geese hunting season combined with float fishing. Above Delta, Colorado, it's always nice to leave winter's early onset at our house at 9,000 feet elevation to revisit summer one more time – or, at the least – to enjoy fall a little while longer.

We used to go cast-n-blast fishing-hunting on the Rio Grande River above South Fork, Colorado and camp in our truck along the bank during mid-October. South Fork has become a lot more developed and regulated since those times and it is harder to find a place that allows this type of freedom along the river anymore due to development. However, after all the many enjoyable times my bun and his buddies fished along the Rio Grande, a fall rendezvous with the river was permanently established in their hearts. Now as married men, these fishing buddies have to select more comfortable accommodations, especially in the crisp chill of fall for the sake of their spouses. One of the Rio Grande fellows bought a house in South Fork, the other simply doesn't go. We turned our sites to the western slope where the Gunnison River is less known (for now) and the fall climate is still rather warm.

In mid-October the Gunnison River below its confluence with the North Fork, which flows from Paonia, is scenic and stunning. The arid desert-like terrain of sandstone cliffs overlooking the river are not baking under the sun in fall, rather the cliffs seem to radiate the summer temperatures, as if caught in time. The river itself is lined by shrubs and cottonwood trees in full fall plumage in October – reds, oranges, yellows, like a scenic postcard.

We like to fish the Gunnison River along its length from Almont above Gunnison to below its confluence with the North Fork above Delta but in the winter, we love the Gunnison River above Delta the most because it is warmer there than on other Colorado winter fishing venues and it is fishable all winter.

Day One: Wires Crossed

Since we were departing for a 10 day trip of meandering with a generally open agenda ("westward bound" being enough of a compass bearing for a starting place, rather than northward, which would mean Montana or eastward, which means Kansas and pheasants, or southward, which would mean were out of our minds and heading for quail or duck near Pueblo....) – we hadn't even made it out of Lake George when we found ourselves stuck for two hours in the asphalt parking lot of a trailer service shop because the electrical system between our truck/camper/ and horse trailer (we were pulling a horse trailer to leave in Grand Junction to be filled with hay on our return trip) was hay-wire and the brakes were not engaging on the trailer without short-circuiting the camper. Two hours in a parking lot. Two....hours......

After the issue was isolated and repaired by the local trailer repair guy the morning was a loss. We examined the option of simply returning home and starting fresh the next day or continuing on westward and hoping to find someplace along the highway to camp. We decided to head out rather than go home because this was the first day of bun's vacation. We headed west but not into the wilderness this time, we chose to take the MAIN highway (I-70, to be exact) rather than our usual meander on lesser traveled highways across the continental divide. We prefer to kind of amble along at our own pace and gawk at the roadside sites of the road less traveled. Due to our late departure, though we needed to get on the main freeway and take it as far as we could while the sun was still up and then look for someplace to camp with the least commitment – someplace along the dreaded I-70 corridor.

Around sunset, were still a couple hours from our horse trailer's destination in Grand Junction so we pulled off at Rifle to spend the night at Rifle Gap Reservoir. Being a cold, windy weekend in October, we knew we the campground would not be very full. As a matter of fact, as evening settled into night we found a site in a nearly loop way up above the reservoir practically all to ourselves expect for one large khaki-fabric cabin-sized hunter's tent - an ATV campsite for elk hunters. We were exhausted and crabby. All we did in the dark was park, feed dogs, pull out camp chairs, and sit in the cold with a beer, not speaking to one another. My 'bun seemed unusually gloomy about the day's lost time, meaning his first day of vacation was a loss in his mind.

We sat in our thick coats in the darkness of that campground and let our bodies settle down from the noise and jostling of the huge Ford diesel engine of the long, stressful day. An enormous full moon began to peek its forehead over the horizon and the Earth's atmosphere produced that optical illusion where the moon seems to be surrealistically big as if in some science fiction movie horror. We watched the moon rise as the dogs finished their dinner and then went off to explore the nearest smells in the night. Eventually, the moon rose over our heads, diminished in size, and cast our shadows in the gravel of the campsite. Bun went to bed so only dogs and I waited until we couldn't stand the cold anymore before we went in the camper to join him. The beauty of the night's moon shadows surrounding us felt too special to leave behind and I wished my bun would have enjoyed them. Eventually, though, my eyes grew heavy and my coat not warm enough to ward off the frigid wind. I vowed to myself that tomorrow I would try to make a better day for my bun's second day of vacation.

Day two: Dogs poisoned.

In Grand Junction, we dropped the horse trailer off next to the field where we were supposed to be picking up bales of hay. The hay was cut but had been rained on, so the farmer flipped it over to let the sun dry it out. The interruption in his hay cutting routine made for a difficult rendezvous for us with our trailer to pick up the hay. Whenever it got dry enough, he would bail it. Then, we would have to come back and pick it up before it rained again. This meant we had to be on call during our cast-n-blast trip and is also the reason we could not bring our dory. We would be wade-fishing for ten days.

It was a relief to drop the long stock trailer off and to be only 21 feet long (we have a really big truck) rather than be almost 40 feet long. All of these little maddening extra assignments (the electrical wiring and the stock trailer drop off) ate into my bun's 10 day vacation. It was already afternoon of the second day of his vacation before we were able to turn our noses to the river.

There is always a good sense of dropping away, dropping into a state of relaxation when one turns off of Highway 50 in Delta to go north up Highway 92 to the turn-off for BLM access to the Gunnison River. Dirt roads make us feel good.

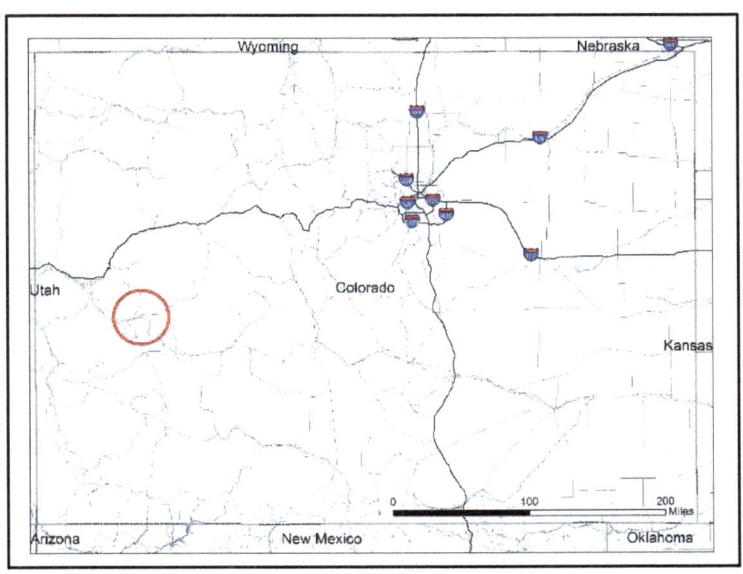

Location of the Gunnison River access above Delta, Colorado.

We followed the dirt road through dismal looking arid, sand hills – roads that wind through - literally - silt and cactus leading to access to the Gunnison River Canyon.

When we finally climbed and peaked over the sandy horizon to see the drop that leads down into the canyon, our stress finally began to melt away. This is really no-man's land in that there is no radio, no cell phone access, and most significantly very few people, if any. Just us, dogs, and... Chukars. There are Chukars in the Gunnison River Canyon! This fact by itself always cheers me up. That said, as we descended into the canyon, the river finally became visible to us and I could see in my huzbun's eyes a happy twinkle. I hadn't seen that in a long time.

Bump bump lurch rocking – that is the road down to the river, especially when in a huge truck with a slide-in camper. The road is a mere trail with huge rocks poking out of the ruts and boulders sticking into the path. The driver has to pay attention and pick places for the wheels to go being mindful of the sides of truck so as to avoid skinning it alive on protruding boulders. The beauty of the colorful autumn plumage along the river was simply stunning. The scenery was enough to make me stop the descent in order to take it all in –sucking in the beauty.

There was no one else in the canyon.

We had our choice of where to fish, where to park, where to camp. I drove past many access points that we were familiar with so that Doug could see the river from different angels and pick which site he wanted to stop at. He directed me over to a set of tracks I hadn't noticed before and we left the dirt road to jostle down to a path to a dead-end under a HUGE cottonwood tree. The river flowed next to us, lined with lush colorful bushes, tall grass, plant varieties I hadn't seen before. I aligned the truck to be perfectly level (a skill I have honed after living out of my slide-in camper for a few months at a time in northern Nevada). When I turned off the loud diesel engine, we all just sat a moment appreciating the stillness of no motion. Silence filled the void of our loud engine now turned off. All of the sudden our dogs leapt to alert and wanted OUT OUT OUT! I open the doors and they all (three) streamed into the afternoon of sun and fun on the river with totally freedom.

Doug went down to the river to check it out for hatch activity and clearness and I began removing things from the camper so I could pop it up.

When Doug returned his eyes were glowing with excitement. He was ready to fish but first he helped me set up the camper and put some of the heavier stuff (like a plastic tub of chopped wood) out under the cottonwood tree. He surprised me when he began to set up our attached awning. We never used it before and these kind of camping luxuries seemed elaborate. We bought the thing as an afterthought. One time we truck camped with a friend in Gila National Forest, New Mexico and thought we were going to die from lack of shade. So, when we saw this awning later we bought it.

Doug fussed and meddled with our camper and gear making white man's camp – a sign of simply enjoying his stuff rather than going fishing right away. I realized he was saving that moment of totally relaxation as a reward. He would put in place our beautiful camp, then totally let go and emerge himself in fishing. Before we left Delta, I had stopped at the last grocery store to buy beer and ice. As an afterthought I snagged a plastic package of raw hide chews for our dogs as a river treat. I gave this to them now and noticed they were oddly reluctant to take them. Very odd indeed. I insisted, though, then Maddie and Elmo took theirs but not Sage. She would have nothing to do with the snacks. Finally, with all the camp in place, Doug retrieved our waders and we sat under the awning in our camping chairs and camping table with beer and snacks to just relax a bit before getting all suited up in our fishing gear.

We noticed that Elmo, who had been running around like a crazy animal in the sand (the "zoomies") as he loved to do, was lying rather tippy next to us. He is an old dog with a white face now. He could hardly hold his eyes open and he was leaning to the side, tipping. We laughed at how tired he was and finished our beer. Then, Doug got suited up and left for the river bank with all the dogs in tow. I noticed that Maddie was also a bit tippy as she struggled to get up and follow the others, kind of listing to the side. When they were gone, I wrapped a tri-tip steak and potatoes in foil and buried that dinner packet in the fire pit. Then, I made a long burning fire to bake our dinner. This would take about 3 hours of slow cooking that way. I like doing this so no one would need to really cook or wash dinner pans later. Dinner would be ready in about 3 hours and I would just hang out to watch the fire and 'putz around' until then, maybe go fishing in the evening.

Shortly after I got the fire going and had our camper completely set-up inside, bun returned and said to me, "*Maddie is tippy*", which as I said I had noticed but did not think anything of that. I looked to see and was alarmed that Maddie came wobbling up from the river like she was really struggling – she was staggering actually, weaving back and forth trying to get one paw in front of the other. I ran to her and both Doug and I lifter her, then carried her to the camper. I thought maybe she got bitten by a venomous snake and I inspected her for such a wound. There were no obvious wounds on her. No swelling or blood.

We had no idea what was wrong.

I listened to her heart, which was beating slow but regularly. Her eyes were not dilated but she did not focus. Her gums were pink and she was breathing really slowly but her breath was strong. In the back of my mind I remembered I has just started a fire and our campsite was entrenched with our gear, we were attached to an awning all set up and it was after 6 p.m. on a Sunday. Going to a vet in town was not realistic.

Then, Doug said, "*Look – Elmo is also tippy!*" and we saw Elmo now also gravely staggering, unable to walk or put one foot in front of the other. He was obviously trying to make it to the camper but he fell and lay in an unnatural heap where he collapsed. We picked him up and put Elmo and Maddie alongside of each other in the lower bed of the camper. Elmo was the same as Maddie – pink gums, slow but steady breath and heartbeat. Pupils not dilated but unable to focus. They lay like dead things where we put them.

"*Could they have gotten into some kind of toxic weed?*" we asked each other. "*Why isn't Sage affected? What did Elmo and Maddie do that Sage didn't*" And all we could come up with was the raw hides. We were reminded that all three dogs were less than enthusiastic about putting their mouths on those treats despite their normal voracious acceptance when offered a raw hide and that Sage refused to hold one at all.

For whatever reason, the raw hides seemed to be the most obvious culprit though we could not rule out a toxic weed or insect – spider or tick – bite. It was also only a couple of weeks before Halloween.

"*I wonder if someone deliberately put a tainted raw hide in the grocery store – the package was not in the dog food aisle – it was hanging in front of my face on one of those hanging displays in another aisle – those kinds of displays that are set up for the spontaneous purchase.*" Doug made a serious face at the possibility of our dogs being the victims of a malicious criminal act targeting an innocent victim – in this case, an innocent animal.

"I don't know...." He said. We didn't want to acknowledge this type of heinous activity would-could occur in a small town like Delta, though we know people are people no matter where you go.

We decided to wait and see how they progressed. We had little choice. They were in a quiet state lying on the bed. They would occasionally adjust their bodies to be more comfortable, which assured me that they were not deteriorating, were rather stable in this altered state. We had no choice really but to wait it out. Doug finished preparing our dinner and I held the two ill dogs all night. In the morning, they both woke us up before the sun rose to have a drink of water. They could get up and down off the bed, then hop back up into the bed. I knew then that they were going to be all right.

Day three: Bun takes on the awning.

In the morning of the third day, both Maddie and Elmo were acting normal again. I rounded up the pieces of raw hide and dug the packaging out of the trash to keep for evidence. In my mind, I intended to pursue this further – to go to the grocery store, to write letters to all the veterinary clinics in Delta, to go to the police. Still it was the third day of our ten-day vacation and we were on the Gunnison River. We should fish if Doug wanted to. We weren't 100 percent sure if the raw hides caused our dogs' illness or if there was some yet to be discovered issue - some other source, such as a nasty toxic weed or some perilous insect – the unanswered questions about how our dogs became so ill put a damper on the idea of fishing in this otherwise lovely spot we had found.

I was enjoying my first cup of coffee, still warming up and keeping an eye on my dogs when our morning conundrum was answered by Mother Nature. I heard the wind come up before it hit us. I was sipping on my coffee hanging out under the cottonwood tree wondering if I should make a morning fire and my bun was just emerging from the camper when the wind hit it broadside. I saw this: My bun's hair, jacket and the awning got scooped up into the air. He stomped down the camper steps as the awning went skyward. A small tornado had engulfed our campsite. The camp chairs flew, the camp table fell over dispensing debris in a swirl and the posts and folding ladder that held the awning went straight up as the wind sucked at our camper.

Doug was grabbing the awning on one side as if he could keep it from flying up. The wind whipped him. The awning tore from its anchor with the camper but only in one half. Doug became a man with a mission. He was surrounded by a whirlwind of destruction and debris. The awning bucked in his arms like it had a life of its own. I hurried to help him with grit in my eyes and I knew I would be of little help against Nature's fury let alone that

I also felt a grip of laughter growing in my chest that I dared not let out.

I watched my huzbun mano-y-mano fight against the wind and awning – a trio locked in battled. Maybe the wind won. I don't know. When the wind left, Doug held half the awning in his arms, we had gear strewn allover kingdom come. The dogs were hiding. Now, we had no excuse for staying at that campsite. We needed to rebuild so we may as well just leave.

In that frame of mind, we decided that between the bad morning and the unknown cause of the dogs' ailment, that we would leave the Gunnison River and head south – head for another river. On the way, we could check in with the hay farmer and go online to check out the potential for raw hide chews making dogs sick.

Prologue

We spent the next seven days fishing a variety of rivers in southwestern Colorado, - the Dolores below McPhee reservoir, the Animas, and then the San Juan in New Mexico. The fishing on the San Juan was so lovely that we stayed four days there. Our hay in Grand Junction was still not ready when we called in so we meandered back toward Grand Junction fishing the Uncompahgre River, visited the Orvis hot springs (no relationship with the fly fishing outfitters) in Ridgway, Colorado. We still had two days to fish before either retrieving hay or going home, so we returned to the Gunnison River late at night and came upon some stranded fishermen in the middle of the night hiking out, but that is another story. That said, we did learn via the internet that there is a possible toxic reaction for dogs with the plastic that is used to wrap raw hide chew toys. In some cases, this reaction has been fatal. In our case, we were lucky that our dogs came out of it and we simply will never buy raw hides wrapped in plastic ever again. We will, however, one day return to the Gunnison Canyon above Delta to hunt chukars and make this a true cast-n-blast retreat to replace our normal fall venue in South Fork.

Gunnison River below the North Fork in mid-October.

Campsite along the willow-lined Gunnison River prior to the wind destroying the awning, prior to the dogs being poisoned, prior to electrical problem swallowing our first day.)

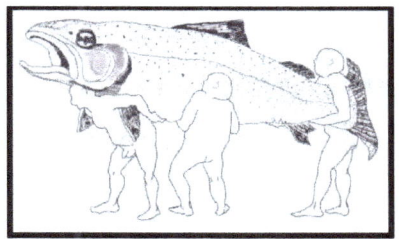

32. River Calves (by Michele White "Murray")

"Animals you come across in the desert are always entities put into the storyline of your life."

Sometimes, you can stumble upon the weather in the northern Nevada surprised as if it's a living thing grazing in a wide pasture. Sometimes, the weather is crossing the road when you drive around the bend. I have caught a glimpse of the weather gently stroking the Mountain. I see the lovely sleeves of God's direct embrace. Clouds and seasons migrate faster than a meandering herd of sheep. One day there will be hot oppressive sun with rattlesnakes under foot and the next day will have a blizzard and freezing wind. One side of the Mountain is May the other is July. December was gone one day and then came again the next day. Sleet can drip from my car and the wind will whip the hood dry as I cross a wide open alluvial valley that is now too hot to wear my coat. The light of the sun from behind gray clouds or peeping above the morning's dew to paint the Mountain's snowy peaks pink and purple can blind you with brilliance and show a myriad of color in the rainbow, or dust devil, or in sun dogs that hang in the sky. The light of the sun is different moment by moment and you can't trust the day's sky to choose your wardrobe. When going to remote areas in northern Nevada, be sure to take shorts, thermal underwear, sunscreen, a rain jacket and extra socks. Take a camera, too, just in case you see something you need to capture to prove it was ever there at all.

The people, animals, and weather are worthy of some kind of story, not just memories to haunt me for a time when I am too old to walk in the wilderness. My huzbun came out to Elko to visit me with our two dogs from Colorado and since it was a rare hot day, we decided to go fly fishing way out in the hills along the Humboldt River east of the Keddy Ranch. You have to hike a bit to get to the river from the road through cactus, cholla, sage and snakes. It's a hot walk with no clue as to the willows and cool water waiting at the end. When we finally arrived at our destination the water was shallow and did not offer much in the way of trout habitat, so we split up to fish in opposite directions. My husband headed downstream, the dogs and I headed up.

The stream was only ankle to knee deep except where it ponded into deep pools are backed up in small eddies. I saw stands of red willow bushes further upstream and hoped their shade might provide cover over one of the deep pools in the bends to provide a habitat for trout to hide in. My hike upstream took me further into the undergrowth with the dogs at my heels, happy to be hiking in the cool water. Eventually, with surprise at one turn in the riparian habitat, I came across a distressed baby calf standing in a shallow eddy struggling to breathe with its head lowered to the water. It seemed to want to drink but couldn't. Something was wrong with its throat.

I told my dogs to stay on the far side of the river and I set my rod down with them. Then, I crossed the stream and slowly approached the calf to examine it for any obvious aliment like rattlesnake bite, broken skin, broken bone, cholla in its mouth, etc. Nothing. The calf allowed me to get close enough to just about touch its face. All of the sudden and without any warning, it turned and slammed me to the ground with a head butt. I scrambled away on my hands and knees and re-crossed the stream to where my dogs were anxiously watching. I was stunned and grateful not to be injured. That was the hardest I had ever been smacked by anything in my life. I appreciated the baby animal's instincts and ability to defend itself even in this distressed state.

I stayed on the far side of the river from the calf to observe it. I watched other cows arrive and climb down from the high bank. They saw the calf and moseyed down the steep path to visit with it. A big orange cow licked the poor orphan who responded with obvious comfort taking a break from beleaguered breathing. Its mother was already dead from having eaten hemlock. The calf thought my dogs and I were waiting for it to drop to its knees so we could prey on it. We weren't. We wanted to help but didn't know what to do and observing its suffering seemed to be some kind of formal ratification or justification for this end to its young life.

It was a beautiful, perfect young animal living in a lovely place and up until this day probably enjoyed the growing wonders of the new spring season. If an animal has to die from one mistake, then this one's death was at the least not so horrible. The day was peaceful on the river. Grass was tall and bushes were leafed out – the first grass and leaves and bugs and song birds this baby animal had ever known. Now, with other cows lowing in the distance, it was slowly asphyxiating from a constricted wind pipe. Probably, its heart was slowing down as well. I wasn't there when the baby died. We left to go find Doug and then we drove to look for help from the nearby Keddy Ranch.

My husband and I left the river and drove to the ranch house to look for ranchers and to tell them of the sick calf. When we got there, we saw adult hippy-looking people sitting in the shade of large leafed-out elm trees weaving baskets. I didn't know until later that this was a ranch my artist friends from Tuscarora come to create their crafts in a sort of art community forum. Doug and I thought it was some kind of resort or halfway house for recovering alcoholics or people suffering mental breakdowns. There was an ambiance of mellow relaxation (creativity) in the air. Later, I learned who they were and that a group of the women went out to investigate the calf but it was already lying dead in the water. They couldn't harvest the calf or cow because hemlock is so toxic that anything that eats it will die. I don't know what the crows will do about that, or the mice.

I think about that calf. That is not the only distressed, dying calf I have entwined with on a river. One summer afternoon, after we had been float fishing for two days on the Rio Grande outside of South Fork, Colorado, Doug pointed across the river from where I was swimming. It was a really hot day and we had been catching a lot of fish so I decided to take a human-and-dog break by swimming in a big clear eddy (with my life vest on). I looked to where Doug pointed. The other side of the river was shallow and cobbles were exposed to make beach. In a pile of driftwood, I saw the white face of a baby calf staring at us. It was watching us humans and dogs have a swim.

"*Awwww, so cute!*" I said, but after we finished our lunch and pushed off, I thought it was rather odd the calf had not budged. There were no other cows in sight.

"*Doug, I think there is something wrong with that calf. It's not right.*" He sighed. I knew that sigh. It was a sigh from the other dying river calf we tried to save in Nevada. As we entered the current I asked Doug if he could please cross the river and land the boat even though it was rocky. I wanted to go see if the calf was stuck or if its mother was around.

Doug obeyed my request as if he was a reluctant sailor following Ferdinand Magellan around the tip of a continent. He did have to haul ass across a river and risk banging the chine of the dory against the cobbles in the current. When he got close enough, I stepped out.

Now, my venture into the brush was probably not as exciting as Doug's. His wife disappeared into the brush. She was gone a long time. We didn't know if there were other cows or even a bull loose in there. The rancher could arrive and get mad at them. She could fall in a hole. All this must have been going on in his mind with the occasional sound of my voice hollering and yelling from the interior. So it was that the bun came looking for me.

I met him half way. We were both looking like explorers in shorts. We were thwacking our way through dense willows in ankle deep mud stepping around cow patties and submerged mossy logs when we ran into each other. I told him,

"There aren't any other cows. The calf was stuck in the pile of driftwood but I got it out. Then, it started hobbling toward the ranch so I followed it. I wanted to be sure it could get to the ranch. Something is wrong with it though. It's breathing like that other calf that died on hemlock."

When we got back to South Fork, I found out the name of the nearest farm and called them. I had to leave a message stating that I found a sick calf and that I put it in a pasture next to a silo on the river and to please let me know if they find it. I worried about the calf too much and decided it must be dead by now. The worst thought I has was that when we first saw it, the baby animal had been suffering not only the terror of being lost from its mother but also suffering from some sort of physical ailment like hemlock poisoning. It had found a nest, a place it felt safe looking over the river, just watching birds, people, and the river pass by. For all the places a dying calf could pick for a final resting place, it had found the most beautiful peaceful place to die. I messed that up.

I regretted my intrusion and clumsy bungling of this animal's final hour. I ruined its peace. It was probably content and comfortable until this human came and terrified it and made it get up and mosey along a path in pain, struggling the whole way. Why did I have to do this? It was for ME, my selfish nature, that I made this decision. I felt miserable about the way I interrupted this animal's peaceful death, moved it away out of its serenity.

The next day on our way home from South Fork, when I got cell coverage again I checked my messages. A man was emotionally telling me thank you over again for finding this calf. They had been looking for it for two days and they had its distressed mother in the barn waiting for it. They went down to the silo, found it, got a veterinarian out there who treated it for a bronchial infection and then they reunited it with its mother. They sent a picture. If Doug hadn't seen that baby in the drift wood across the river and if we decided to float on, it would have died. Thank goodness for a bleeding heart.

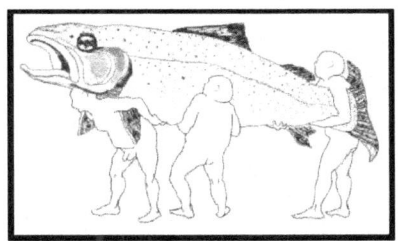

33. Propelled by Desire (by Michele White "Murray")

"Why passion is not the best way to make decisions."

This is the story of what really happened to my propeller. In my world, it is a proven point of fact that I do not mix well with motorized vehicles, especially ones designed to be fast. I should never have bought a motor boat. Every one told me so...

<u>The Propelling Factors</u>

Doug and I float in boats with oars on rivers. At times, we've seen other people with an outboard motor on their river dory boat being propelled upstream on big rivers like the Kootenia River in Montana, and recently we've seen more and more motorized dories on lakes as well. The juxtaposition between operating a classic river-vessel by hand and motor-boating around with other common lake flotilla planted a seed of discontent in my heart, the germination of which was triggered by Ol' Fat Stanley. "OFS" was a chubby accountant in a cubicle in my office and there was nothing interesting at all about him – at first.

Our office parking lot hosted different types of European sport cars and crotch-rocket motorcycles. These sleek,

Italian-looking machines belonged to white-haired guys in the upper echelons of the work force strata. Their fast toys seemed to mock my 18-year old, dented, rusty Subaru station wagon parked next to the dumpsters. My little egg-beater looked like something the Uni-bomber might have driven. People were afraid of parking next to it, like it had some sort of disease. I was standing at the window looking down on all these fast cars, wondering to myself why guys with white hair own all the lovely things when Ol' Fat Stanley interrupted my thoughts to say,

"I feel good today."

"Why?" I asked disinterestedly.

"Because I drove my Porsche to work this morning," he replied.

I turned to see if this was the same person I thought he was. Yes, Ol' Fat Stanley was beaming in front of me. He had a gloating look in his eye. I demanded he take me for a ride right away. We left our desks as if having a job was only a trifle means of passing the day. As I sat back in the leather seats, OFS pulled some expensive sunglasses out of his visor and put them on. Then, he handed me a pair.

"Here, these are guest glasses." I was looking sweet.

He pulled out of the parking lot and headed for the freeway. OFS took me on a long loop that I didn't know existed from our office through the foothills, up into the mountains and back again. At one point, I looked over at the speed-o-meter: "110" said the indicator. NICE... Then, I looked at OFS - he was beginning to actually look kind of sexy to me.

After we got back to the office, I sat at my desk feeling very disturbed. I called my huzbun and asked, "What kind of power car would you like if you could have one?"

"None," he answered very sensibly.

True. My bun does not have a power-car fantasy. He is into boats. However, I was infected by the desire to acquire some new powerful machine: a motorcycle, I thought!

Torque in Motion

While sitting at my desk surfing the Internet for "motorcycles", I accidentally searched on the parameter: "motorboat", because of that alphabetical listing came up before "motorcycle". However, something went "click" in my head when I first saw the image of a blue motor boat. The specifications were, 1978 Sea Hunter, twenty-one feet long with trailer. This was truly love at first-JPEG! I immediately had a vision of myself leaning back in the padded front seat with my hair blowing in the wind reaching for a bag of potato chips, flipping the lid on an ice chest amid a loose pile of inflatable water toys, towels, and fishing rods with kids, dogs and grandparents enjoying themselves. I knew with all my heart that no stinking trolling motor on a river dory would do. I wanted to feel the surge of power from a big engine! I wanted to make a big wake! The blue Sea Hunter in the image had a steering wheel, an awning, a windshield, and a 75-HP engine (1964). I submitted a bid on it and won! Woo Hoo!!! My husband reminded me that you don't "win" in these auctions – you have to pay for it.

The Rake of Fate

We drove to Utah to pick it up. Bun added the expense of this trip to the cost of the boat and calculated the total purchase amount to be around two thousand dollars. I was undaunted. The first weekend with our new boat, the family arrived with all their sea-going gear. Everyone was ready to "go fishing on the lake in Michele's new boat," which we had not yet tested because the motor has to be partially submerged in water in order to run.

My bun was suffering a state of apprehension comparable to embarking on a space mission in a shuttle that was missing a few foam shingles. Kids, grandparents, 2.5 dogs, and multiple bags of potato chips and ice chests got into the big blue thing at the dock before it even slid off the trailer into the water. The sun-screen anointed crew was contentedly sitting with their vests on, sun hats on, rods in hand, in the boat on the trailer as Dale — my bun-in-law — backed the rig down the ramp. Grandparents put unfortunate worms on anxious grandkids' hooks. The sun was already so hot the 2.5 dogs were melting into one sorry poodle on the carpeted floor. Someone was trying to raise the awning and store gear under the seats when the park rangers arrived to check for emergency equipment.

Got life-vests? Check. Fire extinguisher? Check. Emergency paddle? Check. Only 3.2%-alcohol beer? Check. All was perfectly in synch with Colorado State boating regulations. Fishing licenses were on persons. The new registration was in a baggy.

The boat hit the water and floated free of the trailer with the sensation of being airborne. The hull tipped back and forth and the excited jostling crew smiled with wonder as the bun walked the submissive boat on its tether to the end of the dock, then tied it to a loose cleat. Bun-in-law drove the truck up the ramp with trailer dripping like a horse slobbering at the bit and we knew with joy: she floated! She was sea-worthy! This first obstacle went well. I grabbed a skinny kid from behind the steering wheel and flopped my fat butt down in the soft vinyl seat. Dale made his way back to us and hopped aboard.

Bun said to me, "Okay, Michele, turn the engine on!"

With great anticipation everyone suddenly shut-up and held their breath. I turned the key in the ignition and the engine went, "ehhh ehhh ehh ehhhhh, VROOOOOOOM!" and we cheered.

However, my bun was yelling in panic, "Put it in neutral!!!"

He was at the back of the boat by the engine. I was up front at the steering wheel and the boat was yanking at the loose cleat on the dock.

I yelled back, "I am in neutral!"

He was shrieking now, "Put it in neutral-PUT-IT-IN-NEUTRAL!!! No – REVERSE!"

The boat was hammering its hull against the dock. I wiggled the gear lever where the word 'neutral' was hand-written with a magic marker next to the shifter and I repeated,

"I am in neutral! It's already in neutral! It's in neutral-neutral-neutral!"

"No it's not!!" He screamed at me, "I said reverse-reverse-reverse!"

I screamed back at him, "Don't yell at me!"

Then, with both hands held in a horizontal plane like he was trying to sneak up on an injured animal he said in a very controlled, staccato voice reserved especially for men to speak to their wives:

"Honey-the-engine-is-stuck-in-gear-and-you-need-to-put-it-in-neutral-because-we-are-ramming-the-dock..."

By now, all the family members sitting in seats and on ice chests and with fishing rods in hand and vests buttoned up their gills were looking first at one another and then all at me with furrowed brows. So, I said, "Okay, I'll put it in reverse!"

With one mighty yank, the boat lurched backwards out to sea ripping the loose cleat from the dock and knocking everyone to the floor as all 75-horse power went into a backwards drive like a fireball — but only for a moment. Then, it smoothed out going backwards gently. With the boat still floating slowly and the engine running softly, people up-righted themselves, picked up dumped cans of soda and petted the squashed, anxious dogs.

Bun relaxed and said, "OK, Michele. Now, go forward slowly."

I moved the gear shift to the "forward" position, (as designated by magic marker). The motor's pitch changed. People looked calm again and turned their happy faces toward the open-sea where fish were waiting for their worms. The boat continued to smoothly and slowly drift backwards until it finally just wobbled into a loose arc, slightly askew.

The family on our first voyage.

We were adrift! Flotsam! Ship-wrecked! Doomed! The engine was running but with no force! It was then that Dale twisted his cigarette in his fingers, looked over the back end and said,

"*I think we lost Michele's propeller.*"

Immediately, the boat dipped dangerously over on its side because all the occupants leapt to the gunnel to lean their heads over to see and skinny little kids stuck out their skinny little arms to point at the bottom of the lake and the littlest one said, "*There it is!*"

Thrust to Conclusion

For three weeks, my propeller rested at the bottom of the lake in 22.5 feet of water while everyone in the cubicles at work devised plans for its retrieval. Bun and I had gone back multiple times with hooks, baskets, snorkels, wires, and nets.

"*What about a big magnet?*" Old Fat Stanley suggested.

"*It's aluminum,*" I told him and about a million other people with the same suggestion.

We went back every weekend to look at the propeller. We tried several clever schemes with home-made rigs for retrieving the propeller while kids lost their patience and whined at us, "*When are we gonna go fishing?*"

Grandparents who knew better watched from the bank in lawn chairs under umbrellas and flung their bobbers as we dipped and snagged and hovered over the sunken thing.

I learned a lot about propellers that summer. I learned about flukes, diameters, pitch, hub, rake, but especially about cotter pins – in particular, a special type of locking cotter pin that holds the propeller onto the shaft.

By the end of the summer, we had not only mounted a trolling motor on the dory, but I'd also purchased a used-propeller from a dealer in Alaska over the Internet for half the cost of the boat. Now that I am an owner of a fast toy, I know why those guys with the Italian-looking sports cars and rocket bikes have white hair. They have probably left a piece of their heart at the top of a mountain, over the side of a cliff or like me, at the bottom of a lake. That is the cost of being propelled by desire.

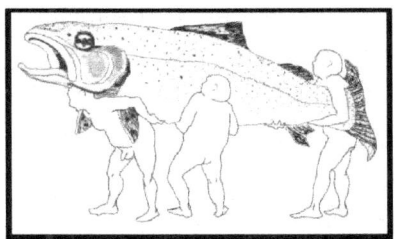

AUTHOR BIOGRAPHIES

Michele White (Murray), Al Marlowe, and Karen Rae Christopherson are geologists, fly fishers, and writers. This trio began when Karen and her sister were researching for their website, www.coloradofishing.net. They discovered Al Marlowe's fly fishing books and realized he was a neighbor and a fellow geologist.

Al Marlowe has been casting flies and lures into streams and lakes all over the West for over 40 years with his lifelong fishing partner/wife, Jean. He's written articles on fishing and outdoor recreation since 1988 and has been published in major outdoors magazines and websites. He has authored two books, "A Hiking and Camping Guide to the Flat Tops Wilderness Area, and "Fly Fishing the Colorado River", and co-authored three eBooks, "Fly Fishing the Flat Tops", "A Fly Fisher's Guide to the North Platte River", and "Fifty Colorado Tailwaters: A Fly Fisher's Guide", with Karen Christopherson. He established Hidden Lakes Press in 2000 to publish fly fishing eBooks. Westwinds Press has republished two of Marlowe's books: "Fly Fishing the Colorado River, A Hiking and Camping Guide to the Flat Tops Wilderness Area", and "Fly Fishing the Flat Tops".

Karen Rae Christopherson began fly fishing in 1970 after taking a fly tying class for a Phys Ed credit at Fairview High School in Boulder. As a geophysicist, Karen has traveled throughout the world with her fly rod. She has written for several fly fishing journals and co-authored multiple maps and books with Al Marlowe. Karen is the webmaster for coloradofishing.net and wyomingfishing.net.

Karen and Al mentored Michele as a writer since 2000. Michele White is a retired international exploration geologist. She owns Tumbling Trout fly shop in Lake George, Colorado and is a professional fly fishing guide. She has been fly fishing and rowing a dory (she is a certified boat handler) on the great rivers of the west for 20 years. Michele is a contributing editor for Mountain Gazette, (thanks to John Fayhee), and has been published in Discover the Outdoors, EQUUS, Fly Fishing World, Native People's Magazine, New Tribal Dawn, and The Aquarian.

Michele stories are included three anthologies:

- "Colorado Mountain Dogs", published by WestWinds Press, 2014;
- "Comeback Wolves: Western Writers Speak for Wolves in the Southern Rockies", published by Johnson Books, 2005; and
- "Hell's Half Mile: River Runners' Tales of Hilarity and Misadventure", published by Breakaway Books, 2004.
-

In addition to her fishing atlas, "Lesser Known Fly Fishing Venues," she also has another book, "Eulogies and Dead Horses", which is a collection of reflective essays about life while fishing and working as geologist all over the world.

www.ingramcontent.com/pod-product-compliance
Lightning Source LLC
Chambersburg PA
CBHW070529010526
44118CB00012B/1088